FRAGILE FREEDOMS

FRAGILE FREEDOMS

The Global Struggle for Human Rights

Edited by Steven Lecce, Neil McArthur,

AND

Arthur Schafer

OXFORD
UNIVERSITY PRESS

OXFORD
UNIVERSITY PRESS

Oxford University Press is a department of the University of Oxford. It furthers
the University's objective of excellence in research, scholarship, and education
by publishing worldwide. Oxford is a registered trade mark of Oxford University
Press in the UK and certain other countries.

Published in the United States of America by Oxford University Press
198 Madison Avenue, New York, NY 10016, United States of America.

© Oxford University Press 2017

All rights reserved. No part of this publication may be reproduced, stored in
a retrieval system, or transmitted, in any form or by any means, without the
prior permission in writing of Oxford University Press, or as expressly permitted
by law, by license, or under terms agreed with the appropriate reproduction
rights organization. Inquiries concerning reproduction outside the scope of the
above should be sent to the Rights Department, Oxford University Press, at the
address above.

You must not circulate this work in any other form
and you must impose this same condition on any acquirer.

CIP data is on file at the Library of Congress
ISBN 978-0-19-022719-7 (pbk); 978-0-19-022718-0 (hbk)

1 3 5 7 9 8 6 4 2

Paperback printed by Webcom, Inc., Canada
Hardback printed by Bridgeport National Bindery, Inc., United States of America

CONTENTS

ACKNOWLEDGMENTS

This book has been a long time in the making and, along the way, we have incurred a number of debts. The greatest, by far, is to our contributors who came to Winnipeg (some, even in the winter!) to deliver insightful talks on such pressing and important topics. We hope they enjoyed the talks, the arguments, and the dinners, as much as we did. The Canadian Museum for Human Rights graciously allowed us to host the Fragile Freedoms lectures in their newly constructed building, even before the museum itself opened to the public. The Canadian Broadcasting Corporation (CBC), which carried all of the lectures on its Ideas program, was a fantastic supporter of our endeavors from beginning to end. We would also like to thank the Asper Foundation, and Gail Asper, in particular, for their generous financial assistance with what ultimately turned into a bigger undertaking than we had originally envisioned. Two of the chapters in this volume reproduce previously published material, and we would like to thank the following institutions for allowing us to do so: chapter 2, Steven Pinker, "A History of Violence" appeared at http://www.edge.org Copyright @ 2011 By Edge Foundation,

Inc. All Rights Reserved; chapter 3, Martha C. Nussbaum (2011) "Capabilities, Entitlements, Rights: Supplementation and Critique", originally appeared in the *Journal of Human Development and Capabilities: A Multi-disciplinary Journal for People-Centered Development*, 12:1, 23–37. Dr. Bryan Peeler helped us with the Index, Heather Hambleton was an expert and efficient copy editor, and Hannah Doyle did an excellent job steering the project into production, as editorial assistant. Thanks also to Cheryl Merritt for production assistance/management.

Steven Lecce would especially like to thank Lucy Randall, our editor, at Oxford University Press (USA) for, by now, *years* of patient, thoughtful, and meticulous support and advice all along the way. This could not have come together in its present form without her.

S.L Winnipeg, 2016

CONTRIBUTORS

Kwame Anthony Appiah is professor of law and philosophy at New York University. He has been elected to the American Academy of Arts and Sciences and the American Philosophical Society and was inducted in 2008 into the American Academy of Arts and Letters. He has served on the boards of the PEN American Center, the National Humanities Center, and the American Academy in Berlin. He has also been a member of the Advisory Board of the United Nations Democracy Fund. Among his recent books are *Cosmopolitanism: Ethics in a World of Strangers* (2006), *Experiments in Ethics* (2008), *The Honor Code: How Moral Revolutions Happen* (2010), *Lines of Descent: W. E. B. Du Bois and the Emergence of Identity* (2014), and *A Decent Respect: Honor in the Lives of People and of Nations* (2015).

John Borrows is Canada Research Chair in Indigenous Law at the University of Victoria Law School. He is the author of *Recovering Canada: The Resurgence of Indigenous Law* (Donald Smiley Award for the best book in Canadian Political Science, 2002), *Canada's*

Indigenous Constitution (Canadian Law and Society Best Book Award, 2011), and *Drawing Out Law: A Spirit's Guide*. Professor Borrows is a fellow of the Academy of Arts, Humanities and Sciences of Canada, Canada's highest academic honor, and a 2012 recipient of the Indigenous Peoples Counsel from the Indigenous Bar Association, for honor and integrity in service to indigenous communities. John is Anishinabe/Ojibway and a member of the Chippewa of the Nawash First Nation in Ontario, Canada.

Anthony Grayling is master of the New College of the Humanities and a supernumerary fellow of St. Anne's College, Oxford. Until 2011 he was professor of philosophy at Birkbeck College, University of London. He has written and edited over thirty books on philosophy and other subjects; among his most recent are *The Good Book, Ideas That Matter, Liberty in the Age of Terror*, and *To Set Prometheus Free*. He is a past chairman of June Fourth, a human rights group concerned with China, and is a representative to the UN Human Rights Council for the International Humanist and Ethical Union. He is a vice president of the British Humanist Association, the patron of the United Kingdom Armed Forces Humanist Association, a patron of Dignity in Dying, and an honorary associate of the National Secular Society. Anthony Grayling's new book, *The Age of Genius*, was published in March 2016.

Germaine Greer has held positions in English literature at the University of Warwick and Newnham College, Cambridge. She is the author of the classic text *The Female Eunuch* (1970). Her other works include *Sex and Destiny: The Politics of Human Fertility* (1984), *The Change: Women, Ageing and the Menopause* (1991), *The Whole Woman* (1999), *Shakespeare's Wife* (2007), and *White Beech: The Rainforest Years* (2013). She owns and finances Stump Cross Books, which publishes the work of seventeenth- and eighteenth-century women poets.

Helena Kennedy, Baroness Kennedy of the Shaws, is currently principal of Mansfield College, Oxford. She is a leading barrister and an expert in human rights law, civil liberties, and constitutional issues. She is a member of the House of Lords and chair of Justice—the British arm of the International Commission of Jurists. She was the chair of Charter 88 from 1992 to 1997, the Human Genetics Commission from 1998 to 2007, and the British Council from 1998 to 2004. She also chaired the Power Inquiry, which reported on the state of British democracy and produced the Power Report in 2006.

Steven Lecce is associate professor of political theory in the Department of Political Studies at the University of Manitoba, where he is also associate dean of arts. His research is primarily concerned with contemporary theories of social and distributive justice, and the ethical bases of the liberal-democratic state. He is the author of *Against Perfectionism: Defending Liberal Neutrality* (2008) and numerous articles about political philosophy. Recently, he was a visiting scholar at Oxford University's Centre for the Study of Social Justice. He is currently completing a sequel to *Against Perfectionism* entitled *Equality's Domain*.

Neil McArthur is director of the Centre for Professional and Applied Ethics and associate professor of philosophy at the University of Manitoba. His publications include *David Hume's Political Theory* (2007). He is currently working in the area of sexual ethics.

Martha Nussbaum is the Ernst Freund Distinguished Service Professor of Law and Ethics, appointed in the philosophy department, law school, and divinity school at the University of Chicago.

Her publications include Aristotle's "De Motu Animalium" (1978), The Fragility of Goodness: Luck and Ethics in Greek Tragedy and Philosophy (1986, updated edition 2000), Love's Knowledge (1990), The Therapy of Desire (1994), Poetic Justice (1996), For Love of Country (1996), Cultivating Humanity: A Classical Defense of Reform in Liberal Education (1997), Sex and Social Justice (1998), Women and Human Development (2000), Upheavals of Thought: The Intelligence of Emotions (2001), Hiding from Humanity: Disgust, Shame, and the Law (2004), Frontiers of Justice: Disability, Nationality, Species Membership (2006), The Clash Within: Democracy, Religious Violence, and India's Future (2007), Liberty of Conscience: In Defense of America's Tradition of Religious Equality (2008), From Disgust to Humanity: Sexual Orientation and Constitutional Law (2010), Not for Profit: Why Democracy Needs the Humanities (2010), and Creating Capabilities: The Human Development Approach (2011).

Steven Pinker is a Johnstone Family Professor in the Department of Psychology at Harvard University. He conducts research on language and cognition; writes for publications such as The New York Times, Time, and The Atlantic; and is the author of ten books, including The Language Instinct, How the Mind Works, The Blank Slate, The Stuff of Thought, The Better Angels of Our Nature, and most recently, The Sense of Style: The Thinking Person's Guide to Writing in the 21st Century. He has served as editor or advisor for numerous scientific, scholarly, media, and humanist organizations, including the American Association the Advancement of Science, the National Science Foundation, the American Academy of Arts and Sciences, the American Psychological Association, and the Linguistic Society of America.

Arthur Schafer is founding director of the Centre for Professional and Applied Ethics at the University of Manitoba. He is a professor in the Department of Philosophy and an Ethics Consultant for the Department of Child Health at the Winnipeg Regional Health Authority. Professor Schafer has published widely in the fields of moral, social, and political philosophy. He is author of *The Buck Stops Here: Reflections on Moral Responsibility, Democratic Accountability and Military Values,* and co-editor of *Ethics and Animal Experimentation.*

FRAGILE FREEDOMS

Introduction

This book originated from a September 2013–May 2014 lecture series meant to inaugurate the Canadian Museum for Human Rights (CMHR). Given even before the museum opened to the public, the talks were the first public events held inside the museum; they were recorded for broadcast on the Canadian Broadcasting Corporation's program *Ideas*. The lectures brought together some of the world's best-known and best-respected thinkers whose work relates to issues of human rights. The lectures did not offer, and did not aspire to offer, any unified vision of human rights, nor a comprehensive survey of human rights as a field. Rather, the series serves to display both the diversity of thinking on the topic and the vitality with which human rights issues are debated and contested.

The CMHR marked something new in Canada: an ideas museum. It was designed not primarily to house artifacts—though it does have some traditional exhibits—but to promote understanding of the concept of human rights and to provoke debate about what that concept means. From the beginning, there was controversy—about the existence of the museum, its cost, and above all, its content. The CMHR opened its doors to the public in the fall of 2014. Planning for the museum began over a decade earlier, in April 2003. Winnipeg businessman and philanthropist Israel Asper, unhappy that the designers of the

Canadian War Museum had decided not to include a Holocaust Gallery, began working on a plan for "an all-inclusive Canadian genocide museum." The original intention was to finance the plan with private funds. Asper died just a few months after announcing the project, and his daughter Gail took over leadership of the initiative. In 2007, Prime Minister Stephen Harper announced that the CMHR would become a federal institution. The government of Canada agreed to cover the operating costs, though funds for the building's construction, which would ultimately exceed $300 million (CND), were divided among the federal, provincial, and municipal governments, and private donors. In exchange for its support, the Canadian government took an active role in designing the museum's contents and remains heavily involved in its operations. There have been allegations that the government has improperly intervened to ensure that the museum presents a sanitized, and therefore inaccurate, version of Canadian history. According to critics, Canada's narrative is depicted in the museum as a steady progression toward even greater enlightenment rather than as a process of ongoing conflict through which oppressed and marginalized groups have struggled for justice, equal status, and recognition.

The museum's location is highly significant and was itself a source of controversy. It occupies a central place at the Forks, an area of Winnipeg so called because it marks the intersection of two rivers, the Assiniboine and the Red. The Forks, which is designated a national historic site, has been a location of documented human activity for six thousand years. Aboriginal peoples used it for centuries as a meeting place, and today many aboriginal people consider it to be a sacred site. The archaeological dig that was conducted in advance of the museum's construction yielded more than 400,000 aboriginal artifacts. However, only 3 percent of the site was excavated, and many people thought the excavation grossly inadequate. Sid Kroker, the archaeologist originally hired by the museum, reported that senior staff at the museum ignored heritage permits and recommendations for "heritage resource management practices" in excavating the site.

The building itself was designed by Antoine Predock, an American architect. It is a massive structure: over twenty-four thousand square meters, the size of four football fields, rising a hundred meters into the air and culminating in an illuminated "Tower of Hope." The museum houses eleven galleries, accessed through what one observer called "an astonishing Escher-inspired labyrinth of ascending, gently inclined walkways, each covered in backlit translucent alabaster imported from Spain." The visitor travels almost a kilometer from the entrance and through the galleries to the top of the Tower of Hope. The guiding ideal is, unabashedly, that of progress: forward and upward, toward freedom and enlightenment. The materials are lavish, and the museum's profile dominates the city's skyline. The building projects not just optimism but confidence in the importance of its mission, and in its own authority to realize it.

From its inception, the CMHR struggled with fundamental issues of definition and scope. Asper's original vision was focused on the commemoration of the Holocaust, and it was always clear that the Holocaust exhibit would occupy a central position. At present, however, there are exhibits devoted to aboriginal rights, to children's rights, to the history of rights in Canada, and to various genocides through history, among other topics. There was fierce debate about precisely what should be included (or not) and how much space should be devoted to each of the various topics that *are* addressed. In the time the museum has been open, it has attracted a large number of visitors and the reviews of its content have generally been positive. However, there is ongoing debate about its direction for the future.

The idea of human rights has a history, though its exact origins are disputed. Some people find it, at least in embryonic form, in the works of Greek and Roman authors, such as Aristotle, Cicero, or the Stoics. Others trace it to various authors writing during the medieval period, while still others insist that the concept only emerges in its recognizable form during the early stages of the Enlightenment. However, there is a general consensus that by the time of John Locke's *Two Treatises of Government*, philosophers had developed something like our modern idea of a human right, or as it was initially called, a *natural* right. Locke and others argued that all human beings, in virtue of their humanity, possess a special dignity, and that this dignity confers upon them protection from certain kinds of oppression.

In Chapter 1, Anthony Grayling makes a bold argument: the true roots of this idea must be sought during the Protestant Reformation. Martin Luther was motivated to rebel against the Catholic Church's authority by his outrage at its excessive luxury and corruption. However, he, along with the Swiss reformers Huldrych Zwingli and John Calvin, demanded not just reform of church practice, as many others before them had done, but also freedom of conscience for all believers. Grayling thinks the impact of this demand for free thought, independent of all authority, transformed the history of Europe. First, it made possible the revolution in scientific thinking that followed hard upon the Protestant Reformation. It also led inexorably to demands for social and political liberty. Once people saw the value of thinking for themselves, they began to expect their governments to provide them with the scope for doing so.

We see the culmination of this broad movement for freedom in the 1780s and 1790s, when the "rights of man" played a central role in motivating the revolutions in America and France. For Grayling, the American and French revolutions were part of the broader movement—the Enlightenment—that established at once both the universality and the diversity of human nature. For Enlightenment thinkers, we all possess a common nature, and we depend upon one another for security and companionship. However, we also possess an innate desire to live our lives in our own ways, free from the dictates of authority. And in order to be free to pursue our particular conceptions of a good life, we must live in a society that is governed by the rule of law and that gives us some form of representation.

Grayling observes that the age of revolution did not achieve the universal freedom of which Enlightenment thinkers dreamed. But the idea of human rights has remained important, as an expression of the sort of society to which we should aspire. Its value has become all too clear in our modern age, when governments have begun to prioritize security at all costs over guarantees of liberty for all. Grayling worries that we now risk reversing the slow but genuine advances toward universal freedom that have been made since Luther's time.

Examining Grayling's provocative thesis on the causal connection between Reformation religious ideas and demands for political freedom, we might observe, as he himself recognizes, that the Protestant leaders were not themselves consistent believers in political or even religious liberty. Reacting to a peasant revolt that challenged the foundation of Germany's social order, Luther wrote that princely authority is divinely ordained, and he explicitly denied that common people are qualified to judge what should be the bounds of their rulers' power. And Calvin suppressed dissenters while in control of Geneva's government, going so far as to allow one of them, Michael Servetus, to be executed. And, apart from the religious ideals of the Reformation, we might find other, concurrent sources for the emergence of the concept of human rights, such as the revival of classical ideas, the spread of literacy, and the economic changes that undermined feudal structures of authority and gave common people more control over their lives. But it is an open question whether any of these could have had a comparable impact under a society still dominated by the iron hand of the Catholic Church.

In Chapter 2, Steven Pinker also takes up the history of human rights, but from a very different perspective. Pinker is concerned not with the ideal but with the empirical reality of how people throughout history have actually experienced violence and oppression, and he asks: Are these perennial and invariant features of human society, or do they change over time? Pinker argues that, when we look carefully at the relevant data, we notice that violence has, in fact, *declined* over time. This is a provocative, powerfully counterintuitive thesis, especially given the widespread sense that the twentieth century— with its multiple world wars, genocides, and regional conflicts— was the *most* violent one in human history.

Pinker argues that, despite the horrific wars that marked it, the twentieth century was demonstrably *less* violent than the earliest stage of human history. For example, forensic archaeology teaches us that around 15 percent of all people alive during the Paleolithic period died from violent trauma. During the twentieth century, by contrast, that number is approximately 3 percent. And it has declined still further since.

For Pinker, these are not anomalies. On the contrary, there has been a steady, measurable decline in violence over the course of human history, and this phenomenon may be traced to a single principal cause: the rise of states. The emergence of states has produced three results, which he terms the pacification process, the civilizing process, and the humanitarian revolution. Thanks to the first, people are less likely to be killed in wars or other inter-social conflicts. Thanks to the second, they are less likely to be murdered by members of their own society. And thanks to the third, they are less likely to suffer violence at the hands of their own governments.

The long decline of violence has reached its culmination during our own era, which Pinker identifies as the one beginning immediately after the Second World War, and which he terms the "long peace." He argues that during this period, the triple forces of democracy, trade, and the emergence of an international community have made people's lives more secure than ever before in history. What Pinker calls the "rights revolution" has also profoundly transformed our society. People are now much less likely to be the victims of racism, sexism, and other forms of prejudice. Children are generally better treated, and animals have now entered the sphere of moral consideration.

Pinker's chapter urges us to move beyond the grim pessimism that often characterizes much contemporary human rights discourse. It is not the case, he says, that nothing ever changes. Human nature does not change. We possess innate violent inclinations. But we also possess contrary, pacific ones. Historical forces determine which come to the fore, and among such forces, ideas figure prominently. Ideology has been one of the great causes of large-scale violence. But at the same time, democratic and cosmopolitan ideals have led us to expand the circle of people with whom we empathize, and whose welfare we want to protect. The civilizing process has progressed in tandem with the spread of literacy and printing, showing that as ideas of freedom and equality are passed on, they have a concrete impact on how society operates.

Pinker concludes that as people become better educated and as progressive ideals continue to spread, violence and prejudice will likely decline still further. His optimism has been challenged both by those who see violence and bigotry as pervasive features of our modern world and by those who think he exaggerates the violence in pre-state and nonstate societies. Such disputes are empirical ones. There are different ways of measuring violence, and reliable data on pre-state and nonstate societies can be elusive. Clearly, people may produce numbers that lead away from Pinker's own conclusions. But he gives us a valuable starting point for the debate.

Critics also point out that Pinker says nothing about the death and suffering that are caused not by violence but by systematic inequality, which deprives many of necessary food and healthcare, and by environmental degradation, which already claims many lives and which promises to claim dramatically increasing numbers of victims in the near future. Pinker readily acknowledges that his thesis concerns violence alone, and that freedom from violence is not sufficient to guarantee people's happiness. However, it is at the very least necessary, and we should not neglect the real impact of its decline, simply because humanity faces other, equally serious challenges.

Finally, critics have contended that Pinker is too complacent about the trend line on violence pointing in a single direction, downward. Even if he is right about the evidence to date, there is nothing to prevent a dramatic reversal. People after the First World War were confident that they had finally "ended all wars."

And modern technology guarantees that future wars, if they occur, have the ability to be vastly more destructive than any in the past. A single global conflict could entirely wipe out the gains of the past centuries. Pinker does not deny this. But he asks us to remember that, whatever challenges we still face, we can draw hope from the evidence that our nature includes, as the title of one of his recent books[1] tells us, "better angels"—innate capacities to live and cooperate peacefully with our fellow humans.

In earlier published work,[2] Martha Nussbaum has argued that there are ten "central capabilities"—fundamental human entitlements—that inhere in the basic idea of social justice. Those capabilities include many of the entitlements also emphasized by the human rights tradition: political liberty, free association, free choice of occupation, and a number of other social and economic rights. For Nussbaum, these capabilities have a close relationship to human rights and, in Chapter 3 she tries to show both how the capabilities approach (CA) clarifies and supplements central aspects of the human rights project and also how, when they are interpreted along CA lines, human rights are *less* vulnerable than they otherwise would be to familiar and frequently made critiques.

How does the CA supplement and clarify the basic notions underlying human rights? As traditionally understood, rights are typically thought to belong to humans (and *only* humans) because people possess some distinctive property or faculty, such as rationality, autonomy, or a sense of justice. This way of grounding

---

1. Steven Pinker, *The Better Angels of Our Nature: Why Violence Has Declined* (New York: Penguin Publishing, 2011).
2. See, for example, "Capabilities and Human Rights," *Fordham Law Review* 66 (1997), 273–300; *Women and Human Development: The Capabilities Approach* (Cambridge: Cambridge University Press, 2000); "Capabilities as Fundamental Entitlements," *Feminist Economics* 9 (2003), 33–59; and *Frontiers of Justice: Disability, Nationality, Species Membership* (Cambridge, MA: Harvard University Press, 2005).

human rights faces a seemingly insurmountable problem, though. Whichever property or faculty is identified as the morally relevant one, people will possess it in *varying* degrees. But then how can we identify a nonarbitrary threshold such that differences below it disqualify nonhuman animals (for example, apes) from having human rights, while differences above it (for example, geniuses as compared to the intellectually disabled) magically yield equal entitlements? In short, what's so magical about *that* threshold? The CA evades this problem by refusing to link fundamental human entitlements to complex capacities like rationality, autonomy, or a moral sense. For Nussbaum, people have rights "in the bare fact of being a living human being: being born from human parents, and having a minimal level of agency or capacity for activity."

The CA also sheds light on the relationship between basic human entitlements and the justification and limits of state authority. Asking which opportunities are entailed by a life that is worthy of human dignity detaches the foundations of human rights from the state. As the social contract tradition teaches us (especially in its Lockean variants), while the *protection* of human rights cannot be reliably undertaken without the state, the *derivation* of those rights is eminently pre-political—people's basic entitlements belong to them independently of, and prior to, membership in an organized political community. The list of central human capabilities, then, is meant to ground and limit the state's authority over its citizens. Under the CA, "it becomes the job of government to secure [the ten basic capabilities], if that government is to be even minimally just."

Finally, the basic capabilities in question are to be understood as "occasions for choice, areas of freedom." Justice only requires that a person have *access* to these opportunities; it does not demand that one actually realize them. Nussbaum concludes that capabilities rather than the associated "functions," as she calls them, should be the central goal of government action because people reasonably disagree about which functions they should choose (or not), so it would be unjust for the state to impose a uniform set of choices or ordering of values.

In these ways, the CA supplements human rights. However, Nussbaum also thinks that the CA yields an internal critique, at least as human rights have sometimes been understood. According to some Enlightenment-based strands of liberal theory, rights can be effectively secured via nothing more than prohibitions of various kinds against state action. On this view, that is, our freedom is guaranteed by the state's doing nothing to impede it. There are (at least) two problems with this idea of so-called negative liberty. First, putatively negative freedoms like freedom of religion and the right to private property always presuppose an expansive, and typically very expensive, state machinery to secure and police them. Second, the narrow focus on the *state* as the sole underwriter or impediment of our freedom ignores how various nonstate entities (corporations, families) and extrapolitical facts (illness, poverty) all profoundly influence our well-being. In reshaping how we conceive of human dignity, then, the CA draws attention to the broader material and social presuppositions of all our rights. At bottom, if we care about social justice, we want an answer to the following question: What are people able to do and be? Sometimes, answering this will involve eminently political (state-centered) facts and values; at other times, not.

Nussbaum's chapter ends by defending the ongoing relevance of human rights language, notwithstanding its supplementation and critique in light of the CA. Human rights discourse is "independently useful and illuminating" because the word "capability" alone does not adequately signal the moral and practical urgency of justice-based entitlements. The idea that capabilities are *not* simply optional needs that may be set aside whenever doing so might promote, say, aggregate wealth "needs to be hammered home in any way we can," and it is precisely the language of human rights that achieves this rhetorical feat: it reminds us that people, simply because they are people, have justified and urgent claims to certain types of treatment, no matter what. While the CA simultaneously supplements and critiques the human rights tradition, we turn our backs on that tradition at our peril.

In Chapter 4, Kwame Anthony Appiah begins by recounting an anecdote about his father's arbitrary imprisonment in the early 1960s at the hands of Ghana's President Nkrumah. Mr. Appiah was incarcerated because of his opposition to Nkrumah's unjust regime, making him one of the earliest prisoners of conscience in Ghana and one of Amnesty International's first cases.

Now, imprisoning people without trial simply for thinking differently is not, as Appiah says, a particularly hard moral case: perpetrators usually know that doing so is wrong, or at least they should, because of the obvious interest we all share in basic freedoms and the protections afforded by the rule of law. However, genuinely hard cases *do* require subtle philosophical analysis, and one of the most promising resources for developing that analysis in connection with the global regime of human rights as articulated in the Universal Declaration of Human Rights (UDHR) is *culture*. Appiah's goal in the chapter is to distinguish between three different but interrelated understandings of "culture"— a term used to denote observable practices, languages, religions, and so on, in a given time and place—to show how, and in what way, those understandings might clarify and motivate the theory and practice of human rights.

First, there is the notion of culture as *identity*—a perspective or self-understanding shared by members of an identifiable group internally unified (but also distinguished from outsiders) by, say, observable practices, languages, religions, and so forth. In this sense, culture lends a somewhat paradoxical aspect to human rights. On the one hand, as the UDHR makes clear, the rights in question are *individual* rights, that is, they protect the interests of separable human beings; on the other, the declaration itself emerged in the shadow of twentieth-century genocide, which also suggests that there is something especially egregious about trying to exterminate people simply because they happen to belong to a particular ethnic, religious, or cultural group.

Beyond genocide, there are the great evils of sexism, racism, homophobia, xenophobia, and religious bigotries of all kinds. These moral blights are unlikely to be either understood or successfully reversed by insisting, as the UDHR does, that, *as individuals*, we all have equal access to fundamental rights regardless of "race, colour, sex, language, religion, political or other opinion, national or social origin, property, birth" or other status. Does it not make more sense, then, to interpret the relevant right-holders in question as the *groups* themselves and, for that reason alone, to abandon the overall framework of the UDHR?

Not necessarily, because, first—as Appiah suggests—even if we are persuaded to endorse collective rights, we might still think that the individual rights set out in the declaration are, for philosophical reasons, *more* fundamental than any collective rights we might contemplate, and second, for political/legal reasons, those collective rights might best be articulated in separate documents. As examples Appiah mentions the UN Convention on the Rights of Persons with Disabilities; the United Nations Declaration on the Rights of Indigenous Persons; and various other UN commissions and conferences against racism, homophobia, and discrimination against the disabled and the elderly. In short, "the issues of group rights some might see as neglected in the UDHR have not always been ignored as a result by the UN or the global human rights community."

Appiah then turns to the *anthropological* sense of culture and asks how it should inform contemporary thinking about social and distributive justice. Here he argues that two prominent Canadian philosophers of multiculturalism—Will Kymlicka[3] and Charles Taylor[4]—move far too quickly from eminently plausible claims about the centrality of cultural membership to individual autonomy and personal identity to the conclusion that the state has not only negative duties of noninterference but also positive duties to support, fund, or in some other way actively protect the viability and vibrancy of cultural groups themselves. Ascribing the state positive obligations to protect human rights to cultural membership (if the interest holders are the *groups* rather than their constitutive members) creates a seemingly intractable problem of definition: cultures are always internally diverse and differentiated, so "who gets to decide which version of the culture is to be sustained"? Appiah maintains that the state must adopt a posture of neutrality[5] toward the at-times-competing cultural ideals of citizens because "taking sides in the disputes within groups about what is and is not worth sustaining . . . will usually violate the government's duty of neutrality."

Finally, there is the notion of culture as *civilization*. Article 27, section 1, of the UDHR says that "everyone has the right freely to participate in the cultural life of the community," and this entails a

---

3. Will Kymlicka, *Liberalism, Community, and Culture* (Oxford: Clarendon Press, 1989).

4. Charles Taylor, *Multiculturalism: Examining the Politics of Recognition* (Princeton, NJ: Princeton University Press, 1994).

5. See Steven Lecce, *Against Perfectionism* (Toronto: University of Toronto Press, 2008) and Jonathan Quong, *Liberalism without Perfection* (Oxford: Oxford University Press, 2011) for comprehensive defenses of this idea.

right "to enjoy the arts and to share in scientific advancement and its benefits." Philosophy, poetry, novels, science, music, painting, sculpture, and the like amount to what Appiah calls "civilization," which has a mutually reinforcing relationship with human rights. On the one hand, many of the rights set out in the UDHR—freedom of religion, freedom of expression, education—make a living civilization possible; "the great monuments of civilization help us to understand what is worth doing in human life and thus empower us to live the lives of dignity that the whole regime of human rights is meant to make possible." On the other, Appiah's moving examples illustrate how civilization both motivates support for and supplies the content of human rights. As he says, without this rich world of civilization, human rights "would be endangered because people would not understand *why* we are entitled to the forms of respect that underlie respect for our rights."

One of Appiah's most provocative claims is that the UDHR is deeply mistaken in interpreting cultural rights in nationalistic rather than in universal terms. The declaration's language suggests that, above all else, people have a fundamental interest in accessing the civilization of *their own* community, and it is *this* access that is supposedly protected by human rights to culture. For Appiah, this particularistic focus is "quite wrong," because while civilization is grounded in particular societies and identities, "it is not the sole possession of the nations and peoples whose members created it." At the heart of Appiah's endorsement of human rights, then, is a cosmopolitan ideal according to which we become more authentic, more faithful to culture as a truly global product and inheritance, the more we transcend our parochial identities and attachments.

In Chapter 5, John Borrows argues that Canadian law must recognize the importance of love in dealing with aboriginal peoples. He says that while the concept seems foreign to the practice of law, it is central to other areas of our lives. Many people involved in public life have love as one of their chief motivations. He points out that many other concepts that are equally abstract and elusive, such as life, liberty, security, equality, and freedom, all have an established place in Western law.

For Borrows, the Canadian government has an obligation to recognize the place of love in the law, because love was a key element in the treaties it made with aboriginal peoples. He cites numerous examples of treaties that use the language of love. Though Borrows does not cite Ronald Dworkin,[6] we can see his argument in broadly Dworkinian terms: Canada's legal and constitutional system, inasmuch as it deals with aboriginal peoples, has embedded within it the concept of love as a moral principle, with a status similar to other abstract ideas such as liberty and equality. As a result, such a principle must guide our interpretation and application of the law. It must also lead us to challenge those laws, such as the Indian Act, that are contrary to a relationship of love between aboriginal peoples and the Crown.

Having explained how the principle of love is already part of Canadian law, Borrows explains how this concept might be applied in one specific area: land and associated resource rights for aboriginal peoples. Aboriginal peoples have a love relationship with the land, and the government should be guided by the need to ensure that that relationship can flourish. This means expanding access to resources beyond the narrow confines of reserves. Above all, it means supporting self-determination for aboriginal peoples both on and off reserve. And love can potentially apply to non-aboriginal people as well. Borrows recommends that we strive to

---

6. See, for example, Ronald Dworkin, *Sovereign Virtue: The Theory and Practice of Equality* (Cambridge, MA: Harvard University Press, 2000).

become "more romantic" when it comes to the earth, especially when considering activities such as fracking, nuclear energy, mining, and logging.

It is striking that Borrows cites with approval treaties that reference the love between colonial powers and aboriginal peoples. Many people would read these references to love as paternalistic or infantilizing. They would also see them as undermining the full recognition of aboriginal rights. As they are traditionally conceived, the rights we possess do not depend on the love of others. That is at least part of the point. Rights can be asserted even against those who despise us, and we may respect the rights of others without feeling a demand to view them with any special affection. However, Borrows may respond that aboriginal rights in Canada require more than just this minimal consideration. As he says, the Supreme Court of Canada has repeatedly affirmed that historic treaties and other rights are to be interpreted in a "large liberal and generous manner." Appealing to love is one way of ensuring that politicians apply such a generous framework to disputed questions.

We might ask whether Borrows's principle of love is limited to the specific question of aboriginal rights. When he discusses love for the earth, however, he seems to suggest that aboriginal people can provide a model for all of us in thinking about our duties toward the environment.

Baroness Helena Kennedy begins Chapter 6 by outlining a series of fundamental transitions that necessitate rethinking the nature and scope of law in a variety of areas: the collapse of the Soviet Union and the birth of fledgling democracies; the enormous technological leaps of late, especially in connection with the internet; the spread of market philosophy and the attendant withering of trade unions; international crime and terrorism; and climate change, to mention a few.

All of this suggests that we are going to need *new* law for twenty-first-century circumstances: "How can we create a web of law that is enabling and not disabling of economic progress and well-being but which prevents abuse and exploitation and instils safeguards for human rights?" We can do so through the regime of human rights, which is, in theory and in practice, precisely a device for the creation of common, international standards. How likely is it, though, that this general framework can be usefully extended to, say, fight international crime, defeat terrorism, and address climate change?

Kennedy points to a paradox at work that threatens the emergence and stabilizing of the requisite norms and practices in these new areas of law. For example, while the increased inequality and resource scarcity caused by climate change is likely to generate *more* regional conflicts as states fight for oil, water, and other precious goods, thus prompting a *greater* need for truly international law, increasingly, people are responding to those threats by seeking "certainty in the politics of identity which leads to ethnic conflict" in the first place.

One of the greatest challenges for legal innovation in responding to all of the radical transformations we are now witnessing, then, is the very nationalism in which people bury themselves to evade or ignore those transformations: "The idea of the nation is being reclaimed with enthusiasm all over the world; people are seeking the comfort of national and religious identity, retiring into smaller and smaller groupings, exhibiting what [has been called] the 'narcissism of minor difference.'" The very globalization that turns us more and more into one world simultaneously drives many of us to withdraw from the international norms and practices that are most appropriate to our shared circumstances: we shelter ourselves from universalism by immersing ourselves in difference. Therein lies one of the greatest threats to human rights.

Kennedy ends her chapter by highlighting some of the reasons we have for optimism about the prospects of legal internationalism, despite the recent trend toward parochialism. In many areas, we *already* have the requisite ideas (human rights) and practices (international courts) so, fundamentally, the problems we face are neither conceptual nor institutional ones. What *is* generally lacking is the political will to give those ideas and practices the preeminence they deserve. If we are to live in a morally decent and safe world, justice must come to displace competing attachments and loyalties.

In Chapter 7, Germaine Greer begins by identifying herself as a liberation feminist, and by distinguishing the ideal of liberation from the ideal of equality. She says that liberation feminism presumes that the world must change fundamentally for both women and men, in contrast with equality feminism, which simply tries to place women and men on equal footing in a world that is otherwise unchanged.

For women, the desire for liberation raises a complicated issue: they must accept that one source of their unfreedom comes from their own bodies. Greer embraces a certain form of gender essentialism. She describes women as "wombed creatures," and she devotes considerable attention to working out the significance of this claim. She says that women's essential natures have been exploited by patriarchy, and that women's bodily integrity has never been protected in law. Women's access to abortion is perpetually under threat, and female genital mutilation remains all too common. There are more subtle attacks on women's bodily integrity as well. Greer catalogues some of the many social pressures that impact on women's experience of their bodies. The result, she says, is a booming industry in cosmetic surgery to allow women to reshape their genitals.

Fundamentally, it is not just women's legal status but the fact that they give birth to children that places women in a unique position. Greer argues that technology now makes it possible for women to be liberated from the need to carry children in their womb in order to be mothers. She says that women may now choose whether or not to continue as wombed creatures. She does not make a case that they should not, but she does urge women to confront this momentous choice not available to previous generations. She presses liberation feminists like herself with a challenge: Should they embrace the opportunity for profound social change that new reproductive technologies present, or does this threaten to deprive them of a vital source of identity and solidarity?

Greer's form of gender essentialism seems to rule out the possibility that transwomen, who do not identify with the gender they were assigned at birth, can achieve the status of true women. Greer embraces this consequence of her position. Her stand on transgender rights was a matter of controversy at the time of her lecture. Challenged on it, Greer defended herself by emphasizing the importance of female-only spaces and argued, controversially, that the invasion of these spaces by transpeople represents an extension of patriarchal domination.

BIBLIOGRAPHY

Dworkin, Ronald. *Sovereign Virtue: The Theory and Practice of Equality*. Cambridge, MA: Harvard University Press, 2000.

Kymlicka, Will. *Liberalism, Community, and Culture*. Oxford: Clarendon Press, 1989.

Lecce, Steven. *Against Perfectionism: Defending Liberal Neutrality*. Toronto: University of Toronto Press, 2008.

Nussbaum, Martha. "Capabilities and Human Rights." *Fordham Law Review* 66 (1997), 273–300.

Nussbaum, Martha. *Women and Human Development: The Capabilities Approach.* Cambridge: Cambridge University Press, 2000.

Nussbaum, Martha. "Capabilities as Fundamental Entitlements." *Feminist Economics* 9 (2003), 33–59.

Nussbaum, Martha. *Frontiers of Justice: Disability, Nationality, Species Membership.* Cambridge, MA: Harvard University Press, 2005.

Pinker, Steven. *The Better Angels of Our Nature: Why Violence Has Declined.* New York: Penguin Publishing, 2001.

Quong, Jonathan. *Liberalism without Perfection.* Oxford: Oxford University Press, 2011.

Taylor, Charles. *Multiculturalism: Examining the Politics of Recognition.* Princeton, NJ: Princeton University Press, 1994.

Chapter 1

Human Rights

Past and Future

ANTHONY GRAYLING

My story about the development of human rights begins in the sixteenth century, with the first modern claim to an important freedom: the freedom to make up one's own mind about matters of great personal moment. The name of Martin Luther is significant in this connection. Mention of his name conjures the image of him attaching his theses to the church door of Wittenberg—the spark that lit the fires of the Reformation, setting off two centuries of bitter religious conflict. It was a conflict that centered on an idea, and ideas, as we know, can be very dangerous. But they also constitute the cogs that drive history onward. The idea in question was that of liberty of conscience. In defending that idea, Luther and his allies sought to undermine the hegemony of the Roman Catholic Church, which for many centuries since the high medieval period had been an immense power over the lives, minds, and polities of Western Christendom.

Before the Reformation, the Roman Catholic Church was effectively an imperial monarchy in Western Europe, and the various kingdoms of that part of Europe were essentially fiefdoms of that monarchy. During the twelfth, thirteenth, and some of the fourteenth centuries, no one was allowed to think differently from the established orthodoxy. Had we lived then, our fates would have been highly circumscribed: We would have lived in a small local area; we would have woken early, worked hard, eaten sparely. Our great moment in the week would have been going to Mass early on Sundays. The walls of our churches would have been graphic novels depicting the doctrines of the Church, and also the admonitions about what would happen to us if we did not obey our priests. We might have even enjoyed these experiences. As all religions (especially Christianity and Islam) have realized, people—particularly young ones—like to be members of communities, dressing up and meeting on regular occasions.

People are also apt to sin. It's a wonderful psychological insight that people want to confess their sins and be absolved. So through the confessional the Church had a useful means of maintaining a hold on people's lives and minds. But that hold also meant that the way people thought about their lives and experiences was limited and essentially impersonal: they lived according to a one-size-fits-all conception of human nature and the value of human life.

Luther was troubled by the fact that in order to raise money to build St. Peter's, the great basilica of Rome, the Church was selling indulgences. By means of them, a person could gain exemption from, say, several million years of purgatory. Luther was outraged by this. He felt that the Church stood between individuals and the deity, and through misinterpretations of scripture and misapplication of its teachings, and by assuming a complete authority over thought, the Church was perverting people's relationship with their

God. That was his chief motivation for attacking the Church's hegemony over thought.

The idea of liberty of conscience, or liberty of thought in religion, then, was the first spark that began a highly consequential process, a process that, once begun, became unstoppable. When people gain liberty of conscience, they want to have liberty of thought in a more general sense. They may want to ask more questions, acquire more information, conduct inquiries, and think about the world more expansively than they did before.

As soon as people have liberty of thought as a more general version of liberty of conscience, they then also want liberty of *action*: they want the freedom to move around more, to travel, to marry whom they please, and to make other important choices that advance their sense of a life worth living, one that feels good to live.

At the same time, increasing liberty of thought allowed the foundations of science to be laid, as well as the foundations of political movements that asked for greater autonomy for the individual. During the age of the Enlightenment, a distinctively modern idea of individual rights and freedoms emerged and flowered in the great American and French revolutions of the eighteenth century.

Luther, Zwingli, and Calvin—the leaders of sixteenth-century reforming movements—wanted to worship, believe, and practice their beliefs in ways that were not prescribed by a central ecclesiastical authority. They (especially Luther) wanted to encourage people to see themselves as having a *direct* relation to a deity and a direct responsibility for *themselves*. As one might imagine, this was enormously important to people genuinely concerned about their eternal prospects. Given the stakes, surely one wants personal control over one's relationship with the deity. So Luther and his early emulators in the reform movement focused on the idea that people should be able to think for themselves—in matters of religion. But, alas, they did not think that people should think for themselves for too long, because when people started to think differently *from them,* they began to worry.

There was indeed a moment in the history of the sixteenth-century Reformation that was crucial in this respect. Michael Servetus, a civil servant in the court of Spain, became interested in the question of the *Conversos,* the Jews who had converted to Christianity. Servetus wondered why, given how otherwise pious and observant the *Conversos* were, they should be excluded from the promises that had been made to the world by the sacrifice of Jesus Christ, simply because they did not accept that Jesus was their savior. He came to think that the problem was that they were not believers in the doctrine of the trinity; they did not see God in the way that Christianity did. He studied the New Testament carefully and found, to his surprise, that the Bible contains nothing about a trinity. Of course it talks about the Father, the Son, and the Holy Ghost, but it does not anywhere say that they are three versions of the *same* person, three in one, the miraculous arithmetic that the Church began to accept as orthodoxy in the fourth century. Servetus reasoned that if only he could persuade fellows in other religions that there is only one God, maybe he could get everyone to agree, thus ending divisions between religions and sects. He wrote a tract passionately criticizing the doctrine of the trinity. He thought this was a great moment and believed that people were being misled about the nature of the Godhead. From Servetus's point of view, the controversy was not simply about peace between religions but rather about the proper path to salvation. He sent his tract to Calvin in Geneva, and Calvin returned the favor, sending Servetus some of his own theological writings, with the intention of correcting what he saw as Servetus's severely inaccurate and indeed heretical view. Servetus, disappointed and annoyed, made the mistake of writing rude comments in the margin of Calvin's book and sending it back. Reportedly, Calvin warned that if Servetus ever came to Geneva, he would not leave it alive.

This was a key moment. The reformers wanted to think for themselves but denied others that right unless they shared their beliefs. In effect, the message was this: think for yourselves, only do *not* disagree with us! Servetus made the mistake of going to Geneva anyway. He was arrested and ultimately burned at the stake—Calvin was one of his chief prosecutors. The episode outraged many followers of the reformed sects, especially a man called Castellio, a celebrated writer of beautiful Ciceronian Latin prose who had been commissioned by Calvin to translate passages of the Bible into Latin for use in school. (These texts were used for hundreds of years, even into the twentieth century, as models of good Latin.) Castellio had thus been Calvin's friend and colleague until Servetus's persecution. In response to that unfortunate episode, Castellio wrote a document that became famous in Europe. With great clarity and force, he unmasked Calvin's hypocrisy: Calvin denied to others the very liberty of conscience that he wanted for himself—unless that liberty was exercised in a manner that pleased him. In Castellio's view, because—as Calvin himself rightly pointed out—the ability to think, believe, and make choices for oneself is so important, *everyone* should be entitled to do so.

Thus, Castellio reprised an argument Erasmus had used much earlier. In effect, Erasmus had said, "In matters of theology we should leave it up to the deity to deal with people if they get it wrong, after they are dead; why don't we just live with each other in peace now? Peace, but not divine punishment, is within *our* power." During the sixteenth century there was a vexing debate about what one needed to know in order to be saved. Some people pointed out that the good thief, attached to one of the crosses beside Jesus, was saved that very day, and because of his brief communication with Jesus. This was putative evidence that, in principle, salvation was attainable for all, and by simple and direct means. Did one really have to plow through heavy volumes of theology in order to save one's soul? Castellio himself made this point. He said, essentially, "Either we leave it up to the deity to decide what is right or wrong, or we go with the assumption that there is something very simple and elemental about what it is that people can and should believe, and ultimately, this is something for them to decide for themselves." Castellio's pamphlet was widely disseminated in Europe and many people endorsed it. This was a key moment for the emerging idea of liberty of conscience.

At about the same time, Copernicus published his account of the way that the heavenly bodies move. Copernicus revived the heliocentric view of the universe partly because of how it simplified mathematical problems in describing the activities of the heavenly bodies. The Church could not accept this because, after all, the foundations of the earth had been laid by the deity and were accordingly fixed forever (see the Psalms, Joshua, and elsewhere in Scripture). Clearly, planet earth was the center of the universe and the others just went around it—Copernicus had to be wrong. Copernicus himself was careful to say that his work was purely theoretical. He wasn't claiming that the sun was indeed the center, only that thinking so made mathematical problems easier to solve. But others, such as Giordano Bruno and Galileo, accepted the theory as true. In fact, most reasonable people privately did so. But saying so publicly was another matter: Bruno was burned to death in the Campo de' Fiori in Rome in 1600 due to his acceptance of the Copernican view, among other things.

The Church correctly perceived liberty of conscience, and religious liberty specifically, as a threat. Once begun, however, the process was unstoppable. The seventeenth and eighteenth centuries witnessed a great efflorescence of inquiry and thought. The scientific revolution of the seventeenth century would not have been possible without a general freeing of the mind for inquiry. From liberty of conscience to liberty of thought and inquiry the step was a very short one. In a further short while it had begun to produce radically different ways of thinking about the world. As I noted earlier, free inquiry inexorably led to social and political inquiry too—liberty of *conscience* developed into liberty of *thought*, which developed into a desire for liberty of *action*. People wanted to make an important change in the way things were organized in society and government.

This process was like water overflowing the banks of a river; it ran into so many different debates and fields. Another significant (but unfortunately now somewhat forgotten) figure was Antony Benezet. He was born in France to a persecuted Huguenot family that fled to England. Benezet then came to North America as a young man and proved to be a brilliant teacher. At night he taught the children of Negro slaves the same things he taught white children during the day. On the basis of this experience, he concluded that the young slave children were no different in any respect from white children: they were every bit as intelligent and curious. By this time in his life Benezet had become a Quaker, and he asked his fellow Quakers why, in light of their beliefs, they continued to support an institution as horrific as slavery. His inquiries into scripture revealed far too much intellectual laxity in then-current thinking about the enslavement of one person by another: How could this practice possibly be morally acceptable? He challenged his fellow Quakers to rethink it. Remember, this was in the middle of the eighteenth century. Once people began to be interested in the questionable morality of slavery—a long overdue change in thinking—it also occurred to them that there were other forms of slavery: the slavery of the worker in the factory, the slavery of the woman in the kitchen, and so on. People began to demand enfranchisement on these fronts as well, in long and laborious processes that ran through the nineteenth and twentieth centuries, and still continue—because discrimination of all kinds persists, even in the advanced countries of the Western world.

Thus the ideas of liberty and the autonomy of the individual proliferated and flourished within a relatively short period, beginning with the Reformation and continuing with the Enlightenment. From the Lutheran movement to, say, the great documents of the French Revolution, a short time passed, but already people were thinking of rights and liberties in connection with a whole range of concerns that we are now familiar with today.

It was the Enlightenment itself that was the greatest impetus to this change. The French Revolution's Declaration of the Rights of Man is a short document that simply says that individuals should be free, free in the sense that they are not owned by anybody else and are not obliged to live their lives under someone else's control. This called into question the hegemony over mind and body previously exercised by both the Church and absolute monarchs. In light of the concepts of equality and freedom, institutions that claimed such authority over people's lives were not entitled to it. So revolution was justified. The point of these emerging ideas of fundamental rights was to open a space around individuals so that they could, if they were energetic and determined enough, create a self-chosen life worth living.

During the American Revolution there was a debate about what should be added to the Constitution in the way of rights protections. People had not thought seriously before about whether or not documents of a constitutional nature should explicitly specify the rights of people. The Federalist Papers' authors asked: Should there be an amendment to the Constitution that protects freedom of expression? Their opponents asked: Why are such explicit protections necessary? Because no one reasonably assumes that the state has the authority to prevent people from expressing themselves, there is no need to guarantee a positive right to that effect. There was also a worry that by conceiving of freedom of expression as a positive (rather than natural) right, one ran the risk of empowering some future government or dispensation to take it away. In any event, the Federalists won the debate, and the First Amendment has become an important part of American constitutional life.

Whether or not you think that specifying or enumerating positive rights in this way is a good idea, one thing it did accomplish was to make the rights in question *concrete*. Previously, people debated various positions about, say, slavery, political conscience, or free inquiry. But before the Enlightenment no one had tried to defend or to tabulate progressive positions by appeal to fundamental rights and liberties. This was a critical turning point in the history of Western ideas: in order for human individuals to have a chance to use their native talents and, by doing so, to live good, fruitful lives, they *must* be autonomous. Life cannot be lived at the dictate of an authority, as though there were only one kind of good life for all of us.

The Enlightenment recognized two complementary and mutually reinforcing truths. First, we share a common nature—we are essentially social creatures. We need to be part of communities, we need to give and receive friendship and affection, and we rely on the support of other people. These are some of our fundamental needs. None of us (or very few of us anyway) likes to be lonely, cold or hungry, tortured, or in pain, or abandoned and neglected when we are in pain and in need of comfort. Second, despite these underlying commonalities, human nature is also a highly pluralistic thing.

What might be a good and satisfying life for you might not be so for me. People make choices, have tastes and interests, and experience needs and desires that differ very widely from one another. What we need, then, is sympathy and generosity in our understanding of other people. We need to have tolerance and recognize that others have an entitlement, a claim on us to be allowed to look for the good in their own way, just as they must allow us to look for the good in our own way.

This kind of mutual recognition necessitates dialogue. Acknowledging difference yields a requirement to converse with one another about how we navigate it. How do we create a society or an order of politics where this great diversity of interests, needs, and practices will not generate conflict?

The idea of individual autonomy went hand and hand with the idea of an objective rule of law, and with a society that was not under a monarch's arbitrary rule. Political rule was consistent with equal freedom only if it was based upon the consent of members of society and was structured so that those members also understood how it worked. This enabled people to adjust their differences with one another and get along. Toleration, freedom, stability, and civil peace—these were the great gifts the Enlightenment promised, and such gifts were thought to be essential preconditions of a plausible answer to Socrates's challenge. Over two thousand years ago, Socrates asked us to think about what sort of people we should be, and what kinds of lives we should lead if we are to live well. By establishing the centrality of liberty to ethics, the Enlightenment gave philosophical expression to the common saying "Different strokes for different folks"—the monolithic society ruled by one hegemonic conception of the good life became unjustifiable. Freedom of thought and action became a central aspect of human flourishing. The documents of the French and American revolutions codify a list of things that people must have—as entitlements—if they are to lead flourishing, rather than wasted, human lives. And they are entitled to those things for no reason other than that they are human beings.

A thinker who was among the earliest to recognize the significance of autonomy as encapsulated in the idea of human rights was John Stuart Mill. In his classic essay *On Liberty*, he argued that there was a more dangerous form of tyranny even than political tyranny, and this was the tyranny of majority opinion over individuals and minorities. He lived in the high Victorian period when repressive and puritanical attitudes in matters of morality were a severely constricting influence on personal freedoms and affections. His argument was that there should be maximum freedom in these respects, consistently with the harm principle, which—to paraphrase—states, "Do not harm others in the pursuit of your own good." His point was that the existence of many and various experiments in how human lives and relationships might be conducted could only conduce to overall human good, and therefore the maximum freedom consistent with the harm principle should be embraced.

Sadly, two centuries intervened after those revolutions before the nations of the world got together in a single body, the United Nations, to affirm their commitment to those ideals in the statement of intent embodied in the Universal Declaration of Human Rights (1948). In the meantime, the world saw real spectacles of horror: for example, the terrible atrocities of the Stalinist purges and the Holocaust in the Second World War. Against the backdrop of such atrocities, the declaration had little trouble commanding widespread assent. It advances a set of rights that, when you reflect upon them even for just a moment, has as its main purpose the protection of a space in which a person, a man or woman, can think freely about things, make choices, and act in ways that feel good, consistent with the good of others and their interests. These were important steps for humanity to take: guaranteeing the equality of men and women, protecting liberty of conscience, protecting privacy and personal autonomy. Together, these rights and freedoms are aspirational. Individuals and societies alike are encouraged to strive to incorporate them so that each person, in his or her own way, might answer Socrates's ethical challenge: What sort of person will you be?

In Plato's dialogue *Meno*, a young man of that name comes to Athens on business from another city. In the evening he goes to hear Socrates lecture. Meno has a burning question to ask the philosopher: Is virtue teachable? Can upstanding citizens pass on their sense of virtue to their offspring? Presumably, ancient teenagers were then as now drinking too much, staying out late, getting pregnant, stealing chariots and doing wheelies around the city walls, and so on. Meno wants to know why civilized Greeks cannot teach their children to behave better. To Meno's great surprise, Socrates says he does not have an answer to this question, because he lacks the answer to an even more fundamental question implicit in the original query: *What is virtue?* What follows is a familiar series of Socratic arguments and counterarguments that ultimately lead Meno into confusion and despair of ever finding the truth of the matter. I tell my students this story to illustrate what I take to be a key point—confusion can be the beginning of wisdom. Socrates was applying this lesson to Meno. He wanted the young man to look at his assumptions and then to think for himself.

Bertrand Russell once said, "Most people would rather die than think, and most people do." The challenge to think is a significant one, but it is also not obvious how one is to do it. Imagine that you take Socrates's challenge seriously: you decide to think about your values and evaluate your philosophical assumptions at five o'clock next Wednesday afternoon (having put yourself, say, into a Rodin-like posture). Then what? First, a blank might ensue, followed by the thought that you have forgotten to get such and such from the supermarket. It's not obvious how to conduct critical reflection in the face of life's distractions. Some of us are lucky—we are paid salaries to be philosophically reflective. When we do this well, we read about other people's ideas, we think carefully about them, we debate, we examine ourselves and our assumptions, we try to work things out, and we have the honesty and integrity to change our minds when better ideas than our own come along.

This critical self-assessment—personal and in the broadest sense political—is what the Enlightenment thinkers saw as essential to both human flourishing and state legitimacy. I have tried to show the link between human rights and the ethical imperative posed by Socrates's challenge. The reason why the rights and liberties enumerated in, for example, documents such as the UDHR, the US Bill of Rights, and the US Constitution, are so important is that they are tools of an ethical life—their intent is to free people to do that all-important task of thinking about a life worth living. If we lacked that important freedom, the moral point behind the idea of rights would be unintelligible, and it would not matter if an imposed orthodoxy prevented people from sorting out life's challenges for themselves. Are human rights unduly paternalistic then? Do they *force* people to lead sometimes painfully reflective and self-critical lives? No, because all they require is that we agree to the following conditional: *if* a person does want to think for himself or herself and to choose a life, he or she should be permitted to do so. And the chosen life might, after all, be thoroughly conventional. This is the bottom line for thinking about rights and liberties. Socrates himself said, "The unexamined life is not worth living." If you live the life that you have not chosen, then you are a ball in someone else's game; you are going in the direction that someone has kicked you in. Of course, you can only think thoughts and make choices for yourself if you are free to do so. This is ultimately why rights matter.

We live in a very tense moment in history. We have embraced technologies that make us naked to the view of anyone who wants to come into our lives, our emails, texts, and smartphones. Search engines watch and then target us with advertisements. Security agencies use these same technologies, and others too, with software that trawls communications, with human intelligence agencies becoming involved if anything looks out of order.

We have embraced these technologies though, strictly speaking, they are not essential to us. We love the internet—in an instant, we can have almost any data we like. Sometimes, this can be a liberating thing. But we also know that the internet is the biggest lavatory wall the world has ever seen, covered in graffiti—so much nonsense, so much falsehood. More than this, it exposes us to scrutiny by government and non-government agencies alike. This is the Faustian bargain that we have made to get the conveniences that new technologies afford us. At times, that bargain compromises our privacy and to some extent our autonomy.

A much more important matter is that our sophisticated democracies have begun to think to themselves that it's not just the high duty of government to protect us from threats but that it's the *first* duty of government. The minute that a government thinks this, it is on the path to limiting our freedoms, our liberties, and our privacy. On the putative tension between liberty and security, Benjamin Franklin correctly thought that "anyone who would trade liberty for security deserves neither." Why? Because as the great Enlightenment figures sought to show, liberty really does occupy a privileged place in the order of values. It allows individuals to choose lives that, to them, are worth living. No government can ever absolutely guarantee our safety, so it is a mistake to assume that in sacrificing our liberty for our safety we have made a reasonable bargain. Life is always full of risk, and liberty is no different—it has costs. We must be mature in this realization and thereby recognize that liberty, in the end, is far more important than simply being safe. Of course we *want* to be safe and it *is* a high duty of government to keep us safe, but safety is not worth much if you are not also free. The rights and civil liberties that allegedly compete with national security are valuable because they allow us to choose lives that permit positive answers to Socrates's ethical challenge. Given this, the standard liberty versus security dilemma is falsely conceived.

When we talk about human rights and civil liberties, when we talk about the world that we occupy now, we should remember a striking fact, and it is this: every one of us lives the life, has the possibilities, and makes the choices that only the most wealthy and powerful aristocrats did four hundred years ago. We all live now as lords because we have those freedoms and we can make those choices. And it would not be fair or just to all those who struggled for all those centuries just gone, nor would we be doing ourselves any favors, still less any favors to our children and grandchildren, if we gave up any of those hard-won liberties and rights thinking that, by doing so, we would be safer and better off. We most emphatically would not be. That is the true purport of a concept of the greatest world-historical significance: the concept of human rights.

Chapter 2

A History of Violence

STEVEN PINKER

Believe it or not—and I know most people do not—violence has been in decline over long stretches of time, and we may be living in the most peaceful time in our species' existence. The decline of violence, to be sure, has not been steady; it has not brought violence down to zero (to put it mildly); and it is not guaranteed to continue. But I hope to convince you that it's a persistent historical development, visible on scales from millennia to years, from the waging of wars and perpetration of genocides to the spanking of children and the treatment of animals.

I'm going to present six major historical declines of violence. In each case, I will cite their immediate causes in terms of what historians have told us are the likely historical antecedents in that era, and then speculate on their ultimate causes in terms of general historical forces acting on human nature.

The first major decline of violence I call the "pacification process." Until about five thousand years ago, humans lived in anarchy without central government. What was life like in this state of nature? This is a question that thinkers have speculated on for centuries, most prominently Hobbes, who famously said that in a state of nature "the life of man is solitary, poor, nasty, brutish and short." A century later he was countered by Jean Jacques Rousseau, who said, "Nothing could be more gentle than man in his primitive state."

In reality, both of these gentlemen were talking through their hats: They had no idea what life was like in a state of nature. But today we can do better, because there are two sources of evidence of what rates of violence were like in pre-state societies. One is forensic archaeology. You can think of it as "CSI Paleolithic." What proportion of prehistoric skeletons have signs of violent trauma, such as bashed-in skulls, decapitated skeletons, femurs with bronze arrowheads embedded in them, and mummies found with ropes around their necks?

There are twenty archaeological samples that I know of for which these analyses have been done. I've plotted here (see figure 1) the percentage of deaths due to violent trauma. They range as high as 60 percent, and the average is a little bit more than 15 percent.

Let's compare that rate with those of modern states, and let's stack the deck against modernity by picking one of the most violent eras that we can think of. This is the United States and Europe in the twentieth century. This is the entire world in the twentieth century—and I've thrown in not only the wars but also the genocides and the man-made famines. It's about 3 percent, compared to the 15 percent rate in pre-state societies. The far right bar in the graph shows the first decade of the twenty-first century. The bar in the graph would be less than a pixel, about 0.03 percent.

The other method of measuring violence in pre-state societies is ethnographic vital statistics. What is the rate of death by violence in people who have recently lived outside of state control, namely hunter-gatherers, hunter-horticulturalists, and other tribal groups?

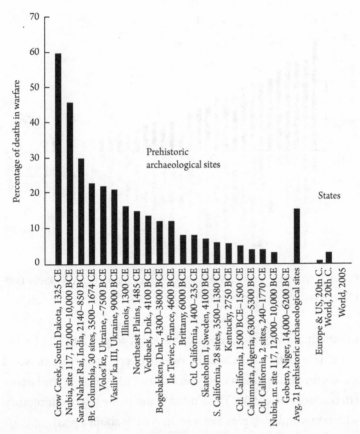

Figure 1. Violent Deaths in Prehistoric Societies. *Sources: Bowles 2009; Keeley 1996; White 2011; Human Security Report Project 2008.*

As far as I know, there are twenty-seven samples for which ethnographic demographers have done the calculation. I've plotted them as war deaths per 100,000 people per year (see figure 2). They go as high as 1,500, but the average across these twenty-seven nonstate societies is a little bit more than 500. Again, let's stack the deck against modernity by picking some of the most violent modern societies for comparison, such as, for example, Germany in the

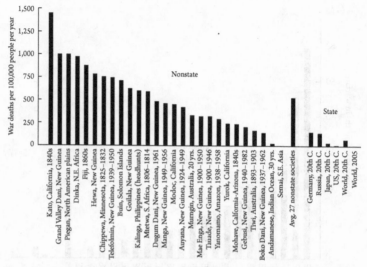

Figure 2. Violent Deaths in Nonstate Societies. *Sources: Gat 2006; Keeley 1996; White 2011; Human Security Project Report 2008.*

twentieth century: its rate is around 135, compared to 524 for the nonstate societies. Russia in the twentieth century, with two world wars, a revolution, and a civil war, is about 130. Japan in the twentieth century is about 30. The United States in the twentieth century, with two world wars plus five wars in Asia, is about a pixel.

As for the world as a whole in the twentieth century, the death rate from all wars, genocides, and man-made famines is about 60 per 100,000 people. The last bar shows the world in the first decade of the twenty-first century; again, it is far shorter than one pixel.

So, not to put too fine a point on it, but when it comes to life in a state of nature, Hobbes was right and Rousseau was wrong.

What was the immediate cause? It was almost certainly the rise and expansion of states. Anyone who is familiar with world history knows about the various paxes—the pax Romana, pax Islamica, pax Hispanica, and so on. It's the historian's term for the phenomenon in which, when a state expands or an empire imposes hegemony over a territory, they try to stamp out tribal raiding and feuding. That is what drives the statistics down.

It's not that these early states had any benevolent interest in the welfare of their subjects but rather that tribal raiding and feuding is a nuisance to imperial overlords. For the same reason that a farmer will take steps to prevent the cattle from killing each other—it's a dead loss to the farmer—imperial overlords tend to frown on tribal battles that just shuffle resources and destroy the tax base.

The second major historical decline of violence can be captured in this woodcut of a typical day in the Middle Ages (see figure 3). The decline has been called the "civilizing process."

It's best illustrated by looking at homicide statistics, which go back to the thirteenth century in many parts of Europe. The

Figure 3. A Day in the Life of the Middle Ages.

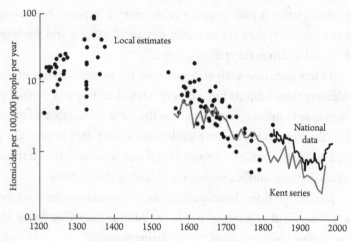

Figure 4. Homicide in England 1200–2000. *Source: Eisner 2003.*

historical criminologist Manual Eisner has assembled every esti-
mate that he could find of homicide rates from records in England
going back to about 1200.

I've plotted them in figure 4 on a logarithmic scale, so that the
scale goes from 100 homicides per 100,000 people per year, to 10,
to 1, to 1/10 of a homicide. And as you can see, there's an almost
two order-of-magnitude decline in homicides from the Middle
Ages to the present.

So a contemporary Englishman has about a fiftyfold less chance
of being murdered than his compatriot in the Middle Ages. (By
the way, this high point of 100 per 100,000 per year comes from
Oxford.)

This is a phenomenon that is not restricted to England. It is
true of every European country for which statistics are available.
Again, here is a logarithmic scale, and the homicide rates go from
between 10 and 100 down to a very narrow window of about 1 per
100,000 per year (see figure 5).

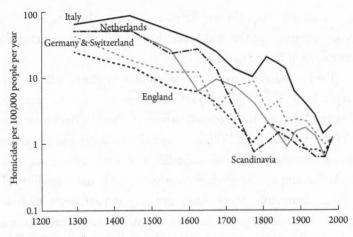

Figure 5. Homicide in Europe, 1300–2000. *Source: Eisner 2003.*

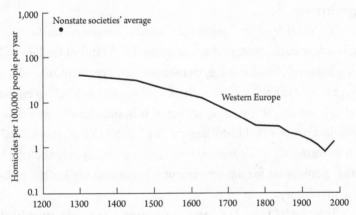

Figure 6. Homicide in Western Europe Compared to Nonstate Societies, 1300–2000. *Source: Eisner 2003.*

Figure 6 shows the average homicide rate of the five Western European regions since the Middle Ages. And just to connect it to the previous historical development, I've plotted the nonstate societies average as well, which is about 500 per 100,000 per year. (This gap is what I called the pacification process.) Then the civilizing process consists of this additional thirty- to fiftyfold reduction in the rate of homicide to the present.

The immediate cause was first identified by Norbert Elias in his classic book *The Civilizing Process*, from which I got the name for this development. In the transition from the Middle Ages to modernity there was a consolidation of centralized states and kingdoms throughout Europe. Criminal justice was nationalized, and warlords, feuding, and brigandage were replaced by "the king's justice."

Simultaneously, there was a growing infrastructure of commerce: a development of the institutions of money and finance, and of technologies of transportation and time keeping. The result was to shift the incentive structure from zero-sum plunder to positive-sum trade.

The third historical decline of violence pertains to the fact that those first states, though they did bring down rates of feuding and vendetta and blood revenge, were rather nasty contraptions, which kept people in a state of awe with techniques such as breaking on the wheel, burning at the stake, sawing in half, impalement, and clawing. In a process that historians call the "humanitarian revolution," these forms of institutionalized violence were eventually abolished. The momentum for this movement was concentrated in the eighteenth century.

This graph (figure 7) shows the abolition of judicial torture (that is, torture as a form of punishment) in the major countries of the day, including the famous prohibition of cruel and unusual punishment by the Eighth Amendment to the US Constitution.

Also during this period there was a reduction in the use of the death penalty for non-lethal crimes. In eighteenth-century England there were 222 capital offenses on the books, including poaching, counterfeiting, robbing a rabbit warren, being in the company of

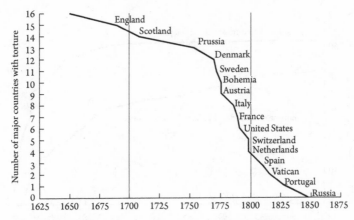

Figure 7. Abolition of Judicial Torture. *Sources: Hunt 2007; Mannix 1964.*

gypsies, and "strong evidence of malice in a child seven to 14 years of age." By 1861 the number of capital crimes was down to four.

Similarly, in the United States in the seventeenth and eighteenth centuries, the death penalty was prescribed and used for theft, sodomy, bestiality, adultery, witchcraft, concealing birth, slave revolt, counterfeiting, and horse theft. We have statistics for capital punishment in the United States since colonial times. As you can see, in the seventeenth century, a majority of executions were for crimes other than homicide. In current times, the only crime that is punished by capital punishment other than homicide is conspiracy to commit homicide.

The death penalty itself, of course, has been abolished in most of Europe. Most of the abolitions were concentrated in the last fifty years. Figure 8 shows the number of European countries with capital punishment. Currently, only Russia and Belarus have it on the books.

But interestingly, even before capital punishment was abolished by the stroke of a pen, it had fallen into disuse. You can see that the

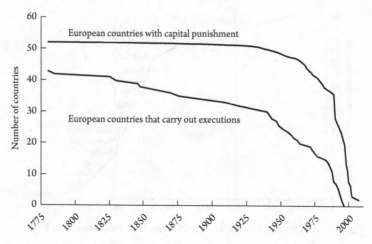

Figure 8. Abolition of the Death Penalty in Europe.

percentage of European countries that actually carried out executions has always been far lower than those countries that had it on the books, and the decline began much earlier.

Now the United States, notoriously, is the only Western democracy that has capital punishment (though only in two-thirds of the states). And to say that the United States has the death penalty is a bit of a fiction. If you look at the number of executions as a proportion of the population, it has been plunging since colonial times (see figure 9). Today, out of about 16,500 homicides per year, there are about fifty executions, and that rate has been in decline as well.

Other abolitions during the humanitarian revolution include witch hunts, religious persecution, dueling, blood sports, debtors prisons, and—of course, most famously—slavery.

Figure 10 shows the cumulative number of countries that abolished slavery. For the first time in history, slavery is illegal everywhere in the world. The last countries to abolish it were Saudi Arabia in 1962, and Mauritania in 1980.

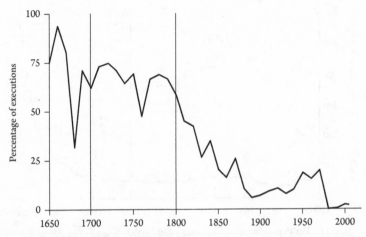

Figure 9. American Executions for Crimes Other than Murder, 1650–2002.
Sources: Espy and Smykla 2002; Death Penalty Information Center 2010.

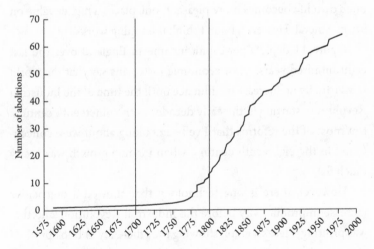

Figure 10. Abolition of Slavery.

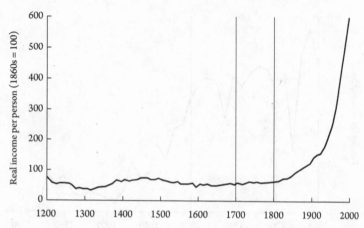

Figure 11. Per-capita Income, England, 1220–2000. *Source: Clark 2007.*

What were the immediate causes of the humanitarian revolution? A plausible first guess is affluence. One might surmise that as one's own life becomes more pleasant, one places a higher value on life in general. However, I don't think the timing works.

Figure 11 depicts per-capita income in England over the last eight hundred years. Most economic historians say that the world saw virtually no increase in affluence until the time of the Industrial Revolution, starting in the early decades of the nineteenth century. But most of the reforms that I've been talking about were concentrated in the eighteenth century, when income growth was pretty much flat.

However, there is one technology that showed a precocious increase in productivity before the Industrial Revolution, and that was printing. Here's a graph showing the efficiency in book production, which increased twenty-five-fold by 1700 (see figure 12). The efficiency was put into use and resulted in exponential growth in books published per year in England, France, and other Western European countries.

Figure 12. Efficiency in Book Production, 1470–1870. *Source: Clark 2007.*

And there were more literate people around to read them. By the eighteenth century, a majority of men in England were literate. Why should literacy matter? A number of the causes are summed up by the term "Enlightenment." For one thing, knowledge replaced superstition and ignorance: such beliefs as Jews poison wells, heretics go to hell, witches cause crop failures, children are possessed, and Africans are brutish. As Voltaire said, "Those who can make you believe absurdities can make you commit atrocities."

Also, literacy gives rise to cosmopolitanism. It is plausible that the reading of history, journalism, and fiction puts people into the habit of inhabiting other peoples' minds, which could increase empathy and therefore make cruelty less appealing. This is a point I'll return to later in the talk.

The fourth historical decline of violence has been called the "long peace." It speaks to the widespread belief that the twentieth century was the most violent in history, which would seem to go against everything that I've said so far. Peculiarly, one never sees, in any of the claims that the twentieth century was the most violent in history, any numbers from any century other than the twentieth.

There's no question that there was a lot of violence in the twentieth century. But take, for comparison, the so-called peaceful nineteenth century. That "peaceful" century had the Napoleonic wars, with four million deaths; the Taiping Rebellion in China, by far the worst civil war in history, with twenty million deaths; the worst war in American history, the Civil War; the reign of Shaka Zulu in southern Africa, resulting in one to two million deaths; the war of the Triple Alliance, which is probably the most destructive interstate war in history in terms of percentage of the population killed, namely 60 percent of Paraguay; the African slave-raiding wars (no one has any idea what the death toll was); and of course, imperial wars in Africa, Asia, and the South Pacific.

These remarks are all qualitative, meant to damp down the tendency to think that just because there was a span of several decades without war in Europe that the world as a whole was peaceful in the nineteenth century.

Now, it is undoubtedly true that the Second World War was the deadliest event in human history in terms of number of lives lost. But it's *not* so clear that it was the deadliest event in terms of percentage of the world population. Here is a graph that I've adapted from a forthcoming book by Matthew White entitled *The Great Big Book of Horrible Things: The Definitive Chronicle of History's 100 Worst Atrocities*. White calls himself an "atrocitologist." He tries to fit numbers to wars, genocides, and man-made famines throughout history.

Here we see 2,500 years of human history, with White's top hundred atrocities, which I have scaled by the estimated size of the world population at the time (see figure 13). As you can see, World War II just barely makes the top ten. There are many events more

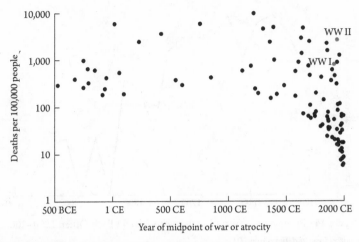

Figure 13. The 100 Worst Wars and Atrocities, 500 BCE–2000 CE. *Source: White 2011.*

deadly than World War I. And events which killed from 0.1 percent of the population of the world to 10 percent were pretty much evenly sprinkled over 2,500 years of history.

Now this funnel-like concentration of points in the last few centuries does *not* mean that in ancient times they only committed big atrocities, whereas now we commit both big and little atrocities. It's rather an artifact of "historical myopia": the closer you get to the present, the more information you have. The smaller atrocities in the past were trees falling in the forest with no one to hear them, or not even deemed worthy of being written down.

Let's zoom in now on the last five hundred years. There is a data set from Jack Levy on trends in great-power war. These are wars that involved the eight-hundred-pound gorillas of the day, that is, the countries that could project military power outside their boundaries, which account for a disproportionate amount of the damage due to war (because wars fall along a power law distribution of damage).

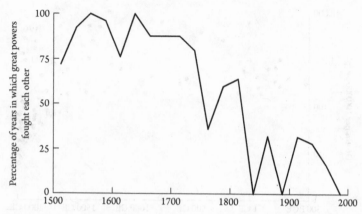

Figure 14. Proportion of Years Great Powers Fought Each Other, 1500–2000.
Source: Levy and Thompson 2011.

Figure 14 shows the percentage of time that the great powers were at war. We see that five hundred years ago, the great powers were pretty much *always* at war with one another, and then the proportion of each quarter-century filled with great-power wars declined steadily.

But now we see a graph of the deadliness of war, which shows a trend that goes in the opposite direction—though wars involving great powers were fewer in number, they did more damage per country per year (see figure 15). Even that trend, though, did an about-face after 1950, when for the first time in modern history, great-power wars became simultaneously fewer in number, shorter in duration, *and* less deadly per unit of time.

Now let's zoom in on the last century, the twentieth century. Figure 16 shows deaths in wars all over the world, not just those involving the great powers. It shows that the increase in deadliness of war did indeed result in two horrific spikes of bloodletting centered on the two world wars. But since then there has been a long stretch without that degree of bloodletting. The fact that the

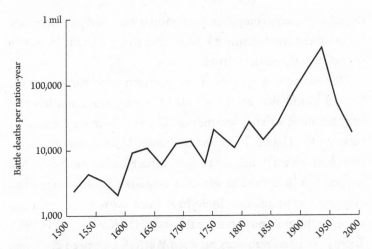

Figure 15. Deadliness of Wars Involving a Great Power, 1500–2000. *Sources: Levy 1983; Correlates of War Project, PRIO.*

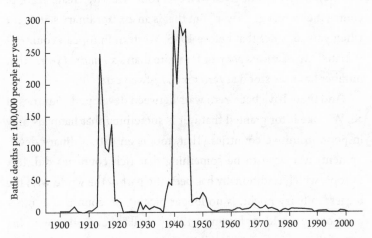

Figure 16. Deaths in War, 1900–2000. *Source: Lacina, Gleditsch, and Russett 2006.*

twentieth century comprises one hundred years, not just fifty years, is one of the reasons why it's misleading to say that the twentieth century was the most violent in history.

The extraordinary sixty-five-year stretch since the end of the Second World War has been called the long peace and has perhaps the most striking statistics of all: zero. There were zero wars between the United States and the Soviet Union (the two superpowers of the era), contrary to every expert prediction. No nuclear weapon has been used in war since Nagasaki, again, confounding everyone's expectations. There have been no wars between any subset of the great powers since the end of the Korean War in 1953. There have been zero wars between Western European countries. The extraordinary thing about this fact is how unextraordinary it sounds. If I say I'm going to predict that in my lifetime France and Germany will not go to war, everyone will say, "Yeah, yeah; of course they won't go to war." But that is an extraordinary statement when you consider that before 1945, Western European countries initiated *two new wars per year* for more than *six hundred years*. That number has now stood at zero for sixty-five years.

And there have been zero wars between developed countries at all. We take it for granted that war is something that happens only in poor, primitive countries. That, too, is an extraordinary development; war used to be something that rich countries did, too. Europe, which traditionally has been the part of the world with the biggest military might, is no longer picking on countries in other parts of the world, or hurling artillery shells at one other with the rest of the world suffering collateral damage. This change has been extraordinary.

Now, what about the rest of the world? What has happened in the other continents while Europe has been racking up its peaceful zeros?

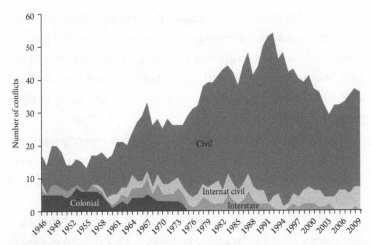

Figure 17. Number of Wars, 1946–2008. *Sources: UCDP/PRIO; Human Security Report Project.*

First let's look at the number of wars. These graphs start at 1946, and they span the entire globe (see figure 17). I'll divide it into the different categories of war.

One kind of war has vanished off the face of the earth. The colonial war, which used to be quite destructive, no longer exists, because the European powers have given up their colonies. (This is, by the way, a stacked layer graph, so the relevant visual variable is the thickness of the layers.)

Here we see the fate of interstate wars, wars between two sovereign states. These have also been dwindling since the end of the Second World War. However, the number of civil wars—both pure civil wars within a country and internationalized civil wars, where some foreign country butts in, usually on the side of the government defending itself against an insurgency—increased until about 1990, and then has shown somewhat of a decrease as well.

Since 1946 there have been fewer wars between states but more civil wars, mainly because newly independent states with inept governments have been challenged by insurgent movements, and the Cold War powers armed both sides. But even civil wars declined after 1991 with the end of the Cold War and the stoking of these proxy wars by the superpowers.

The crucial question now is this: What kills more people, the fewer number of wars between countries, or the greater number of wars within countries? Figure 18 shows the deadliness (number of people killed per year of war) of interstate wars since the 1950s.

The tall bars represent deaths in interstate wars, and they have plummeted over the decades. Much shorter are the internationalized civil wars and the civil wars. The fact that we have more civil wars and fewer interstate wars means that the total number of

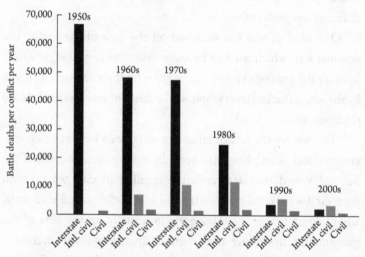

Figure 18. Deadliness of Interstate and Civil Wars, 1950–2005. *Sources: UCDP/ PRIO; Human Security Report Project.*

people killed has gone down, because the interstate wars of the past killed far more people than the civil wars of the present.

Now let's put the numbers back together, and instead of looking at the number of *wars*, look at number of *deaths*, again scaled by world population (see figure 19). This stacked layer graph shows the number of people killed in wars since 1946. There are the colonial wars, and the interstate wars, with spikes corresponding to the eras of the Korean War, the Vietnam War, and the Iran/Iraq War. These are the numbers of people killed in civil wars and internationalized civil wars.

The trajectory has been bumpy, to be sure, but we are actually living in a time that even in comparison to recent decades is comparatively peaceable. In fact, one could almost say that the dream of the 1960s folk singers is coming true in the first decade of the twenty-first century: The world is putting an end to war.

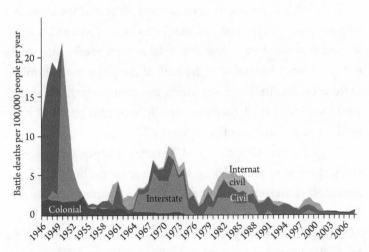

Figure 19. Battle Deaths in Wars, 1946–2008. *Sources: UCDP/PRIO; Human Security Report Project.*

What about genocide? The last couple of graphs plot what are called "state-based conflicts," in which you have two organized armed forces fighting, and at least one of them is a government. What about cases in which governments kill their own citizens? Again, there's a cliché that the twentieth century was the "age of genocide." But the claim is never made with any systemic comparison of previous centuries.

Historians who have tried to track genocide over the centuries are unanimous that the notion that the twentieth was a century of genocide is a myth. Frank Chalk and Kurt Jonassohn, in their *The History and Sociology of Genocide*, write, "Genocide has been practiced in all regions of the world and during all periods in history."

What did change during the twentieth century was that for the first time people started to *care* about genocide. It's the century in which the word "genocide" was coined and in which genocide was first considered a bad thing, something to be denied instead of boasted about.

As Chalk and Jonassohn say of ancient histories, "We know that empires have disappeared and that cities were destroyed, and we suspect that some wars were genocidal in their results. But we do not know what happened to the bulk of the populations involved in these events. Their fate was simply too unimportant. When they were mentioned at all, they were usually lumped together with the herds of ox and sheep and other livestock."

To give some examples, if Old Testament history were taken literally, there were genocides on almost every page: the Amalakites, Amarites, Canaanites, Hivites, Hitites, Jevasites, Midianites, Parazites, and many others. Genocides were also committed by the Athenians in Melos; by the Romans in Carthage; and during the Mongol invasions, the Crusades, the European wars of religion, and the colonization of the Americas, Africa, and Australia.

We have something even resembling numbers only for the twentieth century. But if we plot those numbers, they refute the impression that the massacres in Bosnia, Rwanda, and Darfur are indications that nothing has changed, that the world has learned nothing since the Holocaust. This graph shows the best estimates that we can find of rates of death in genocide. Is certainly true that there was a burst of genocides from the 1930s to the early 1950s in Europe, and from the 1920s through the 1970s in Asia. But the trend since World War II has been downward. It is definitely *not* the case that "nothing has changed" since the era of the Second World War. Even counting the Rwandan genocide, a small proportion of the world's population today, compared to earlier decades, is massacred by their governments.

So what are the immediate causes of the long peace, and what I call the new peace (that is, the post–Cold War era)? They were anticipated by Immanuel Kant in his remarkable 1795 essay, "Perpetual Peace," in which he suggested that democracy, trade, and an international community were pacifying forces. The hypothesis has been taken up again by a pair of political scientists, Bruce Russett and John Oneal, who have shown that all three forces increased in the second half of the twentieth century. In a set of regression analyses, they showed that all of them are statistical predictors of peace, holding everything else constant.

Specifically, the number of democracies has increased since the Second World War, and again since the end of the Cold War, relative to the number of autocracies. There's been a steady increase in international trade since the end of the Second World War. There's been a continuous increase in the number of intergovernmental organizations that countries have entered into. And especially since the end of the Cold War in 1990, there's been an increase in the number of international peacekeeping missions, and even more importantly, in the number of international peacekeepers that have kept themselves between warring nations, primarily in the developing world.

The final historical development I call the "rights revolutions." This is the reduction of systemic violence at smaller scales against vulnerable populations such as racial minorities, women, children, homosexuals, and animals.

The civil rights revolution saw a reduction in the once socially sanctioned practice of lynching. There used to be 150 lynchings per year in the United States; over the course of the twentieth century, the number has gone down to zero. Hate crime murders of blacks, which started to be recorded in the mid-1990s, went down from the single digits to one per year. Non-lethal hate crimes such as intimidation and assault have also been in decline since they were first measured.

Also, the kinds of racist attitudes that encourage violence against minorities, such as the percentage of Americans saying that they would move if a black family moved in next door, or believe that black and white students should go to separate schools, has now fallen into the noise—the range of crank opinion—and is basically indistinguishable from zero. This is a trend that has taken place not just in the United States, but worldwide. The number of countries that have laws on the books that discriminate against ethnic, religious, or racial minorities has been in steady decline. In fact, the number of countries that have tried to tilt the scale in the other direction with affirmative action and remedial discrimination policies has increased. More countries in the world now discriminate in favor of disadvantaged minorities than against them.

The women's rights movement has seen an 80 percent reduction in rape since the early 1970s when it was put on the agenda as a feminist issue. There has also been a two-thirds decline in domestic violence and spousal abuse (wife beating), and a 50-percent decline in husband beating. In the most extreme form of domestic violence, namely uxoricide and mariticide, there's been a decline both in the number of wives murdered by their husbands and the number of husbands murdered by their wives. In fact, the decrease is much more dramatic for husbands. Feminism has been very good to men, who are now much more likely to survive a marriage without getting murdered by their wives.

In the United States, the number of states that permit corporal punishment, such as "paddling" and "hiding," in schools has declined. In much of Europe, corporal punishment has been abolished outright. The approval and implementation of spanking have been in decline in every country in which they have been measured. In fact, spanking—even by parents—is now illegal in many European countries. Here are data from the United States, New Zealand, and Sweden. Child abuse, too, has been in decline since statistics were first recorded in the early 1990s. And violence in schools, such as fighting and bullying, has also decreased.

The gay rights movement has seen an increase in the number of states in the world that have decriminalized homosexuality (it used to be a felony). Anti-gay attitudes, such as whether homosexuality is "morally wrong," whether it should be made illegal, and whether gay people should be denied equal opportunity have been in steady decline, as have hate against gays.

The animal rights movement has seen a decline in hunting, an increase in vegetarianism, and a decrease in the number of motion pictures in which animals have been harmed.

The key question now is: Why has violence declined over so many different scales of time and magnitude? One possibility is that human nature has changed, and that people have lost their inclinations toward violence. I consider this to be unlikely. For one thing, people continue to take enormous pleasure, and allocate a lot of their disposable income, to consuming simulated violence, such as in murder mysteries, Greek tragedy, Shakespearean dramas, Mel Gibson movies, video games, and hockey.

But perhaps more to the point are studies of homicidal fantasies, which ask people the following question: "Have you ever fantasized about killing someone you don't like?" When you ask that question of a demographic with a very low rate of actual violence, namely American university students, you find that about 15 percent of the women and a third of the men *frequently* fantasize about killing people they don't like, and more than 60 percent of women and three-quarters of men at least *occasionally* fantasize about killing people they don't like. (And the rest of them are lying—or at least might sympathize with Clarence Darrow when he said, "I've never killed a man, but I've taken great pleasure in reading many obituaries.")

A more likely possibility is that human nature comprises inclinations toward violence *and* inclinations that counteract them—what Abraham Lincoln called the "better angels of our nature." Historical circumstances have increasingly favored these peaceable inclinations.

What are the parts of human nature that militate toward violence? I count five, depending on how you lump or split them.

There's raw *exploitation*, that is, seeking something that you want where a living thing happens to be in the way. Examples include rape, plunder, conquest, and the elimination of rivals. There's nothing particularly fancy in the psychology of this kind of violence other than a zeroing out of whatever inclinations would inhibit us from that kind of exploitation.

There's the drive toward *dominance*, both the competition among individuals to be alpha male and the competition among groups for ethnic, racial, national, or religious supremacy or preeminence.

There's the thirst for *revenge*, the kind of moralistic violence that inspires vendettas, rough justice, and cruel punishments.

And then there's *ideology*, which might be the biggest contributor of all (such as in militant religions, nationalism, fascism, Nazism, and communism), leading to large-scale violence via a pernicious cost-benefit analysis. What these ideologies have in common is that they posit a utopia that is infinitely good for infinitely long. You do the math: If the ends are infinitely good, then the means can be arbitrarily violent and you're still on the positive side of the moral ledger. Also, what do you do with people who learn about an infinitely perfect world but nonetheless oppose it? Well, they are arbitrarily evil and deserve arbitrarily severe punishment.

Now let's turn to the brighter side, our so-called better angels. They include the faculty of *self-control*: the ability to anticipate the consequences of behavior and inhibit violent impulses. There's the faculty of *empathy* (more technically, *sympathy*), the ability to feel others' pain. There's the *moral sense*, which comprise a variety of intuitions including tribalism, authority, purity, and fairness. The moral sense actually goes in both directions: It can push people to be more or less violent, depending on how it is deployed. And then there is *reason*, the cognitive faculty that allows us to engage in objective, detached analysis.

Now we face the crucial question: Which historical developments bring out our better angels? I'm going to suggest there are four.

The first implies that Hobbes got it right: A leviathan, namely a state and justice system with a monopoly on legitimate use of violence, can reduce aggregate violence by eliminating the incentives for exploitative attack; by reducing the need for deterrence and vengeance (because leviathan is going to deter your enemies so you don't have to), and by circumventing self-serving biases. One of the major discoveries of social and evolutionary psychology in the past several decades is that people tend to exaggerate their adversary's malevolence and exaggerate their own innocence. Self-serving biases can stoke cycles of revenge when you have two sides, each of them intoxicated with their own sense of rectitude and moral infallibility.

Historical evidence that the leviathan is a major pacifying force includes the first two historical developments that I spoke of, namely the pacifying and civilizing processes, both of which were consequences of the rise of states. Also the fact that reversals in the trends, where violence re-erupts, tend to take place in zones of anarchy (i.e., the American Wild West), failed states, collapsed empires, and mafias and street gangs that deal in contraband (so they can't call in the court system to enforce their interests in business disputes but have to resort to intimidation and revenge). A final kind of evidence is the demonstrable effectiveness of international peacekeepers, who use a kind of soft power on the international stage to keep warring parties apart.

The second pacifying force is identified by the theory of gentle commerce. Plunder is a zero-sum or even a negative sum game: the victors' gain is the loser's loss. Trade, in contrast, is a positive-sum game. (We will hear more from both Leda and Martin that reciprocal altruism, such as gains in trade, can result in both sides being better off after an interaction.) Over the course of history, improvements in technology have allowed goods and ideas to be traded over longer distances, among larger groups of people, and at lower cost—all of which change the incentive structure so that other people become more valuable alive than dead. I doubt that the United States is going to declare war on China (though there's much that we don't like about that country), because they make all our stuff.

And I doubt China will declare war on us, because we owe them too much money.

Some historical evidence comes from statistical studies showing that countries with open economies and greater international trade are less likely to engage in war, host civil wars, or have genocides.

A third pacifying force is what Peter Singer called the "expanding circle," although Charles Darwin in first stated the idea in *The Descent of Man*. According to this theory, evolution bequeathed us with a sense of empathy. That's the good news; the bad news is that by default, we apply it only to a narrow circle of allies and family. But over history, one can see the circle of empathy expanding: from the village to the clan to the tribe to the nation to more recently to other races, both sexes, children, and even other species.

This just begs the question of what expanded the circle. I think one can argue that the forces of cosmopolitanism pushed it outward: Exposure to history, literature, media, journalism, and travel encourages people to adopt the perspective of a real or fictitious other person. Experiments by Daniel Batson and others have shown that reading a person's words indeed leads to an increase in empathy, not just for that person but also for the category that the person represents.

Historical evidence includes the timing of the humanitarian revolution of the eighteenth century, which was preceded by the Republic of Letters, the great increase in written discourse. Similarly, the long peace and rights revolutions in the second half of the twentieth century were simultaneous with the "electronic global village." And perhaps—this is highly speculative—but it's often been stated that the rise of the internet and of social media might have been behind the color revolutions and the Arab Spring of the twenty-first century.

I think the final and perhaps the most profound pacifying force is an "escalator of reason." As literacy, education, and the intensity of public discourse increase, people are encouraged to think more abstractly and more universally, and that will inevitably push in the direction of a reduction of violence. People will be tempted to rise above their parochial vantage point, making it harder to privilege their own interests over those of others. Reason leads to the replacement of a morality based on tribalism, authority, and puritanism with a morality based on fairness and universal rules. And it encourages people to recognize the futility of cycles of violence, and to see violence as a problem to be solved rather than as a contest to be won.

What's the evidence for reason being a pacifying force which has helped to propel the decline of violence? We do know that abstract reasoning abilities (as measured by the most abstract components of an IQ test) have increased in the twentieth century. The so-called Flynn effect consists of an increase of about three IQ points per decade since the beginning of the twentieth century, and the gains have been concentrated not in factual knowledge such as vocabulary and information but in abstract reasoning (similarities questions like, "What do an egg and a seed have in common?" and "What do an inch and a pound have in common.")

It's been shown that people (both at the level of individuals and of entire societies) who have higher levels of education and measured intelligence commit fewer violent crimes; cooperate more in experimental games, have more classically liberal attitudes; are more receptive to democracy, and are less likely to be racist, sexist, xenophobic, or homophobic.

Whatever the causes of the decline of violence, it has profound implications. One of them is it calls for a reorientation of our efforts toward violence reduction from a *moralistic* mindset to an *empirical* mindset. It leads us to ask not just the question "Why is there war?" but—and it might be a better question—"Why is there peace?" Not just "What are we doing wrong?" but "What have we been doing right?" Because we *have* been doing something right, and it seems to me that it's important to understand what it is.

In addition, the decline of violence has implications for our assessment of *modernity*: the centuries-long erosion of family, tribe, tradition, and religion by the forces of individualism, cosmopolitanism, reason, and science.

Now, everyone acknowledges that modernity has given us longer and healthier lives, less ignorance and superstition, and richer experiences. But there is a widespread romantic movement which questions the price. Is it really worth it to have a few years of better health if the price is muggings, terrorism, holocausts, world wars, gulags, and nuclear weapons?

I argue that despite impressions, the long-term trend, though certainly halting and incomplete, is that violence of all kinds is decreasing. This calls for a rehabilitation of a concept of modernity and progress, and for a sense of gratitude for the institutions of civilization and enlightenment that have made it possible.

Chapter 3

Capabilities, Entitlements, Rights

Supplementation and Critique

MARTHA NUSSBAUM

CAPABILITIES AND THE LANGUAGE OF HUMAN RIGHTS

Ten central capabilities, I have argued, are important human entitlements, inherent in the idea of basic social justice.[1] My capabilities list includes many of the entitlements that are also stressed in the human rights movement: political liberties, the freedom of association, the free choice of occupation, and a variety of economic and social rights. And a list of capabilities, like a list of human rights, supplies a moral and humanly rich set of goals for development, in place of the focus on gross domestic product per capita as the single important development goal.

1. Martha Nussbaum, *Women and Human Development: The Capabilities Approach* (Cambridge: Cambridge University Press, 2000); Martha Nussbaum, "Capabilities as Fundamental Entitlements," *Feminist Economics* 9 (2003), 33–59; Martha Nussbaum, *Frontiers of Justice: Disability, Nationality, Species Membership* (Cambridge, MA: Harvard University Press, 2005).

Capabilities, as I understand them, have a close relationship to human rights, as understood in contemporary international discussions. In effect, the capabilities on my list cover the terrain covered by both the so-called first-generation rights (political and civil liberties) and the so-called second-generation rights (economic and social rights). And they play a similar role, providing both a basis for cross-cultural comparison and the theoretical underpinning for basic constitutional principles.

Both Amartya Sen and I connect the capabilities approach (CA) closely to the idea of human rights.[2] In both *Women and Human Development* and *Frontiers of Justice,* I have described the relationship between the two ideas at some length, and I have tried to show how my version of the CA responds to some criticisms frequently made of human rights approaches.[3] For example, feminists have frequently criticized the human rights approach for being male-centered and for not including some abilities and opportunities that are fundamental to women in their struggle for sex equality. They proposed adding to international rights documents such rights as the right to bodily integrity, the right to be free from violence in the home, and the right to be free from sexual harassment in the workplace.[4] My list of capabilities explicitly incorporates that proposal. (Sen's more informal discussion of specific capabilities does so implicitly.) More needs to be done, however, to explain the theoretical reasons for supplementing the language of human rights with the language of capabilities. The aim of this chapter is to clarify the

2. See Amartya Sen, "Elements of a Theory of Human Rights," *Philosophy and Public Affairs* 32 (2004), 315–356.
3. Nussbaum 2000, ch. 1; Nussbaum 2005. See also Martha Nussbaum, "Capabilities and Human Rights," *Fordham Law Review* 66 (1997), 273–300.
4. As I discuss at the end of the "Critique: Positive and Negative, Action and Inaction" section, this situation evolved dramatically in the late 1980s and early 1990s, although the feminist expansion of the terrain of rights remains contested, not least in the United States.

relationship further, in ways that go beyond the analysis offered in my earlier article on the topic.[5]

I view (my version of) the CA as one species of a human rights approach. It supplements other approaches in several useful ways. It also differs from some versions of such an approach, and offers a useful critique of those versions. In some ways, I shall argue, it thus offers significant advantages over all (other) versions. The relationship between capabilities and human rights, then, is one of inclusion but also one of supplementation and critique.

SUPPLEMENTATION: CLARITY ABOUT THE BASIC NOTIONS

The idea of human rights is by no means a crystal-clear idea.[6] Rights have been understood in many different ways, and difficult theoretical questions are frequently obscured by the use of rights language, which can give the illusion of agreement where there is deep philosophical disagreement. People differ about what the *basis* of a rights claim is: rationality, sentience, and mere life have all had their defenders. They differ, too, about whether rights are pre-political or artifacts of laws and institutions. The CA, in my version, has the advantage of taking distinct positions on these disputed issues, while stating clearly what the motivating concerns are and what the goal is.

In my two books about the CA, I argue that the ten central capabilities are fundamental entitlements inherent in the very idea of minimum social justice, or a life worthy of human dignity.[7] Where

5. Nussbaum 1997.
6. See also Sen 2004.
7. Nussbaum 2000, 2005; see also Nussbaum 2003.

humans are concerned, the basis of these entitlements lies not in rationality, nor in any other specific human property, but rather in the bare fact of being a living human being: being born from human parents and having a minimal level of agency or capacity for activity. That is enough to give a human being a dignity that is equal to that of every other human being.[8] Thus, a person in a persistent vegetative state does not have these entitlements, nor does an anencephalic child. But human beings with high levels of mental retardation—unable to use language, unable to move, and so forth—do have them, provided they have some degree of active functioning or striving. In this way, my approach differs from most human rights approaches, which, historically, have grounded entitlements in the possession of rationality and have excluded human beings with severe mental disabilities.[9]

Nor are human beings the only creatures with fundamental entitlements, in my view. I argue that all sentient beings, at least, have entitlements to the basic conditions of a life according to the dignity of their species.[10] So human rights are just one species of rights, and all animals have rights of some sort. Here the CA departs radically from almost all human rights approaches, where the accent is firmly on *human*.

The capabilities on my list are what I call *combined capabilities*, by which I mean the internal preparation for action and choice, plus circumstances that make it possible to exercise that function. For example, the capability of free speech requires not only the ability to speak (that would be an *internal capability*, cultivated through

---

8. Nussbaum 2008.
9. Nussbaum 2005; Martha Nussbaum, "Human Dignity and Political Entitlements," in *Human Dignity and Bioethics: Essays Commissioned by the President's Council on Bioethics* (Washington, DC: US Government Printing Office, 2008), 351–380.
10. Nussbaum 2005.

development and education), but also the actual political and material circumstances in which that ability can be used. Governments do not support the capability of free speech, in the sense required by my list, if they educate people to be eloquent speakers but then deny them the political right to speak freely in public.

Of course human beings have all sorts of capabilities, meaning abilities or opportunities to act and choose. The items on my list, however, are the result of an evaluative argument that asks the question: What opportunities are entailed by the idea of a life worthy of human dignity? The approach, then, does not read capabilities off from a factual observation of human nature as it is. Many capacities inherent in our nature are bad (e.g., the capacity for cruelty), and many are too trivial to be inherent in the idea of a life worthy of human dignity. My approach, then, does not value capabilities as such, or freedom as such. Some freedoms or opportunities to act are good and some bad, some important and some trivial.[11]

These central entitlements are pre-political, belonging to people independently of and prior to membership in a state, and they generate constraints that political institutions must meet if they are to be even minimally just. In other words, these rights belong to humans just on account of their human dignity, and they would exist even if there were no political organization at all, although no doubt they would not be secured to people. The CA in this way takes issue with those human rights approaches that consider rights to be an artifact of laws and institutions.[12] In the absence of a world state (a goal that I do not support), we can speak of duties to secure the capabilities to everyone in the world only if we do think

11. Nussbaum 2003. Sen (2004) seems to grant this point (see pp. 319 and 321); however, I argue in Nussbaum (2003) that in his *Development as Freedom* (New York: Knopf, 1999), Sen treats freedom as an all-purpose good, even something that ought to be maximized.
12. See also Sen 2004.

of them as pre-political in this way. Approaches that make all entitlements the artifact of political organization have a very difficult time justifying redistribution from richer to poorer nations. The CA, then, sees human rights as pre-political, inherent in people's very humanity. This has been overwhelmingly the most common type of human rights theory.

Entitlements are correlative with duties: if people have entitlements, then there is a duty to secure them, even if it is difficult to say to whom the duty belongs.[13] In *Frontiers of Justice*, I argue that the whole world is under a collective obligation to secure the capabilities to all world citizens, even if there is no worldwide political organization. How to assign the duties to specific groups and individuals is a difficult matter, and I attempt to take that on, at least in a preliminary way.[14] The difficulty is greatest in the global context— there is no single overarching state, and no good reasons to think that we ought to have one.. Even here, many of the duties to secure human capabilities are assigned to states, but some belong, as well, to nongovernmental organizations, to corporations, to international organizations, and to individuals.[15] In that sense the duties are ethical rather than political: they do not require a state enforcement mechanism to be morally binding.[16]

Nonetheless, I do not agree with Sen that rights (or the central capabilities) have no conceptual connection to state action.[17] I agree with my American revolutionary ancestors: one key purpose of the state is to secure to people their most central entitlements. As the US Declaration of Independence puts it, recapitulating a long tradition

13. See also Sen 2004, 340–341.
14. Nussbaum 2005, ch. 5.
15. Nussbaum 2005.
16. Nussbaum 2005; cf. Sen 2004.
17. See Sen 2004, 320 and 345–348.

of argument, "To secure these rights, Governments are instituted among Men, deriving their just powers from the consent of the governed"—and any government that fails to secure basic entitlements has failed in its most essential task.[18] If a capability really belongs on the list (or, if a given human right really belongs in a list of human rights), then governments have the obligation to protect and secure it, using law and public policy to achieve this end. The world context is unique, because there is no overarching state, and thus none that can be shown unjust because it flunks this task. When we are thinking of a specific nation-state, however, we are entitled to ask whether it has secured the ten capabilities (the central human rights) to people. If it has not, it is not even minimally just.

Sen attempts to avoid granting a conceptual connection between capabilities and government by citing examples of capabilities (rights) that should not be legally enforced, such as the right of a family member to be consulted in all family decisions.[19] Of this example I would say: either such conduct is required by a notion of a life worthy of human dignity, or it is not. If it is, then it ought to be legally enforced (just as we legally enforce prohibitions on child abuse and domestic violence). If it is not, then it will not belong on a list of central capabilities or human rights. If we do put something on that list, we connect it, both practically and conceptually, to the idea of the purposes for which "governments were instituted among men." My own view is that such matters of consultation are matters concerning which citizens may reasonably disagree, given differences in their comprehensive doctrines, religious and ethical. They should not be coercively enforced, but by the same token they should not be on the capabilities list, which is said to be the

18. US Declaration of Independence, July 4, 1776.
19. Sen 2004, 345.

potential object of an overlapping consensus among all the reasonable comprehensive doctrines.

The ten capabilities, then, are *goals* that fulfill or correspond to people's pre-political entitlements. In the context of a nation, it then becomes the job of government to secure them, if that government is to be even minimally just. In effect, the presence of entitlements gives governments a job to do, and a central job of government will be to secure the capabilities to people. The existence of human and animal lives gives a reason for governments to exist and generates obligations of a distinctly political kind. When, in the case of the whole world, we decide that an overarching single government might not be the best way of solving problems of capability failure in poorer nations, government still plays a major role in securing them: the government of the poorer nations, in the first place, and in the second place, the governments of richer nations, who have obligations to assist the poorer.[20] Giving people what they are entitled to have in virtue of their humanity is a major reason for governments to exist in the first place, and a major job they have once they exist.

The capability goal ought to be set in a way that is realistic for each capability singly, and in a way that promises reasonably coherent deliverance of the whole interlocking set of capabilities. Where we face the need to make tradeoffs, promoting one capability at the expense of another, we ought to say that this is a tragic situation in which minimal justice cannot be done, and we should get to work to produce a future in which all citizens can enjoy all the capabilities. It is reasonable to set the level of each capability quite high, aspirationally; nonetheless, it would be wrong to set the level in a utopian manner, precluding all possibilities of realization. Thus, I basically agree with Sen that human rights, and capabilities so understood,

20. Nussbaum 2005, 5.

should not be thought to be absent because they are at present unrealizable.[21] I would add, however, that the specification has to be responsive to the conditions of human life as it is, and not one that would require a total transformation of the world in order to permit realization. The right way to set the level is a job for judgment and discussion.

When we talk about capabilities as fundamental entitlements, what is the motivating concern? Human rights approaches sometimes leave a blank here, although at times they invoke a notion of human dignity. The dominant intuitive idea is that of waste or starvation. Some lives that people are given are pinched and cramped; they are unable to unfold themselves, to choose, to act, to use key human powers. Their lives are thus not worthy of human dignity. The intuition underlying my version of the approach is that idea of waste or tragedy, coupled with the idea of the inherent dignity of the life of the being in question, which demands better than that. (From now on, putting other animals to one side, I shall speak of human dignity, but it must never be forgotten that this is just one type of dignity that laws and institutions should recognize.)

Why does the task of securing capabilities belong (apart from the global context) to government? I am operating here with a very widespread and basic notion of the purpose of government, one that many nations share all over the world: governments are instituted to secure things to people that they could not secure without government, and governments must be measured by the extent to which they fulfill that task.[22] There are many ways in which governments can secure human capabilities, but I have focused on their

21. Sen 2004, 326.
22. Martha Nussbaum, "Constitutions and Capabilities: 'Perception' against Lofty Formalism," *Harvard Law Review* 121 (2007), 4–97. (Hereafter Nussbaum 2007a)

role in generating accounts of fundamental constitutional entitlements and then securing those entitlements.[23] Thus I would agree with Sen that capabilities need not always be secured by legislation, but I would remark that almost all modern democracies divide these functions among the executive, the judiciary, and the legislature. If I focus on the part that involves constitutional law and its judicial interpretation, this is not to neglect the role of these other branches.[24] There is much more to be written about the relationship between capabilities and political structure, and I hope to attempt this task in the future.

What is the scope of capabilities? Sen holds that the idea of human rights is broader than the idea of capabilities, because both processes and opportunities figure in the idea of human rights, whereas capabilities are concerned with opportunities and not with processes.[25] I am not convinced; indeed, I just do not understand the reasons for this alleged bifurcation. One of the many things that people need to be able to do, if their live are to be worthy of human dignity, is to have access to the legal system on terms of equality with other people; one way this right is often impeded is via asymmetrical procedural hurdles. The due process rights that all modern constitutions guarantee, in a way closely bound up with guarantees of equal protection, are procedural rights, but they are also fundamental opportunities for people to act and be treated as fully equal citizens. Again, one procedural right that most modern democracies treat as salient is the right to privacy, understood as a type of control over one's intimate decisions. That right (fundamental to women's control over their reproductive capacities) is a procedural right, but

23. Nussbaum 2007a.
24. See Sen 2004.
25. Sen 2004, 330–337.

it is also an individual capability or opportunity. Sen says procedural rights differ from others because they involve governmental structure—but so do all the capabilities.

All the central capabilities, like all human rights, are best seen as occasions for choice, areas of freedom. Thus a person can have all ten capabilities on my list without using all of them, and this is true of rights as well. A person may have the right to religious freedom, for example, in a secure form, and care nothing about religion.[26] The central reason why capabilities and not the associated functions are held to be central goals of government is that it would be wrong for government to push people into functioning in these areas, since citizens reasonably differ over which functions they will choose and which they will not. In this way, the CA, like human rights approaches, avoids being "imperialistic" or imposing a single lifestyle on all. Instead, it asks governments to create and protect contexts of choice.

In this section I have gone over some of the ways in which the CA *supplements* human rights approaches: by taking clear positions on these disputed and sometimes ignored questions.

SUPPLEMENTATION: CAPABILITIES ON THE GROUND

There is another way in which the CA usefully supplements the language of human rights: by simply being concrete and close to the ground. The language of rights often strikes people as abstract. The daily question What am I able to do and be? is, by contrast, down-to-earth and practical. It is a question that people in all walks of life

26. See also Sen 2004, 335.

ask themselves every day, even when they do not have any education. It does not require any philosophical grounding to ask and answer this question, nor does it require a formation that is peculiar to one culture rather than another.

Thus, when development practitioners or activists discuss with people what they think they need and should have, the language of capabilities seems like a natural extension of their demands, not like a foreign imposition. The important cross-cultural study of Wolff and de-Shalit shows that new immigrant groups, discussing their disadvantages, gravitate naturally to capabilities language and understand the approach very quickly. They are able to use it to add items that my list does not include, and to add general concepts, such as that of "capability security," which my approach did not foreground.[27] I have heard similar reports from activists in many places.

Throughout my own work on the CA, I have always emphasized this specificity, saying that what is universal in the approach is only a starting point. Each nation must and should describe the capabilities it pursues more concretely, using its own history and traditions as a guide.[28] And even a constitution is likely to be pretty general. The capabilities have to be further specified through both legislation and judicial interpretation, together with the work of administrative agencies.[29] Human rights documents do not typically comment on this interpretive process or perform the further specification of the rights they include (although human rights practitioners do typically perform this work).

Another advantage of using such a down-to-earth language, a language people in nations all over the world use in their daily

27. Jonathan Wolff and Avner de Shalit, *Disadvantage* (New York: Oxford University Press, 2007).

28. Nussbaum 2000, 2005; compare Sen 2004, 323.

29. Nussbaum 2007a.

activities, is that we do not even appear to be imposing a Western construct upon formerly colonized peoples. I do not believe that the idea of human rights is especially Western; it has roots in many traditions.[30] Moreover, the experience of colonial subjects did not show them that any idea of human rights was central to Western culture. For what they saw every day was a blatant disregard of human rights (of freedoms of speech and assembly, of economic entitlements, and many others). When Nehru and Gandhi put rights into the Indian Constitution, they did not see themselves as aping Western powers but rather as constructing bulwarks against what, in their experience, the West had stood for. In recent years, the work of human rights activists in many nations has grounded rights talk in local realities. Nonetheless, if we do not want to waste time responding to the postcolonial critique of rights, which is very widespread in places where people do not know much history, we will get some advantage from focusing on the neutral and international language of what people are actually able to do and be.

Because capabilities language is determinate and down-to-earth, when we are operating within a legal or constitutional framework that uses the language of rights, we still need capabilities language to make clear what it is really to secure the entitlement in question. The right to political participation, the right to religious free exercise, the right of free speech—these and others are all best thought of as secured to people only when the relevant capabilities to function are present. In other words, to secure a right to citizens in these areas is to put them in a position of capability to function in that area. To the extent that rights are used in defining social justice, we should not grant that the society is just unless the capabilities have been effectively achieved. This understanding of rights helps us

30. Sen 1997, 2004, 351–355.

understand what questions judges should be asking when they pose questions about constitutional rights.[31]

Of course people may have a pre-political right to good treatment in this area that has not yet been recognized or implemented. Or it may be recognized formally and yet not implemented. But by defining the securing of rights in terms of capabilities, we make it clear that a people in country C do not really have an effective right to political participation—for example, a right in the sense that matters for judging that the society is a just one— simply because this language exists on paper. They have been given right only if there are effective measures to make people truly capable of political exercise. Women in many nations have a nominal right of political participation without having this right in the sense of capability. For example, they may be threatened with violence should they leave the home. In short, thinking in terms of capability gives us a benchmark as we think about what it is really to secure a right to someone.

Here we are dealing above all with *supplementation*, but we will see that supplementing rights language with that understanding of what it is to secure a right to someone leads directly to a *critique* of some versions of the human rights approach.

CRITIQUE: POSITIVE AND NEGATIVE, ACTION AND INACTION

Securing the central human capabilities, as I describe them in the CA, involves affirmative material and institutional support, not simply a failure to impede. "Combined capabilities" are the goal, and these require the preparation of the material and institutional

---

31. Nussbaum 2007a.

environment (and the education of the person) so that the function in question can actually be selected.

We see here a major advantage of the CA over understandings of rights—very influential and widespread—that derive from the tradition within liberalism that is now called "neoliberal," for which a key idea is that of negative liberty. The idea of negative liberty is frequently traced back to the work of Isaiah Berlin, but his subtle categories are often ill-understood, and I do not want to digress in order to pursue the correct interpretation of his work, since I am interested in contesting the libertarian or neoliberal understanding of rights that borrows this term.

Often fundamental entitlements have been understood as nothing more than prohibitions against interfering state action. If the state keeps its hands off, those rights are taken to have been secured; the state has no further affirmative task. Indeed, if one reads the US Constitution, one sees this conception directly, for negative phrasing concerning state action predominates, as in the First Amendment:

> Congress shall make no law respecting an establishment of religion, or prohibiting the free exercise thereof; or abridging the freedom of speech, or of the press; or the right of the people peaceably to assemble, and petition the Government for a redress of grievances.

Similarly, the Fourteenth Amendment's all-important guarantees are also stated in terms of what the state may not do:

> No State shall make or enforce any law which shall abridge the privileges or immunities of citizens of the United States; nor shall any State deprive any person of life, liberty, or property,

without due process of law; nor deny to any person within its jurisdiction the equal protection of the laws.

This phraseology, deriving from the Enlightenment tradition of negative liberty, leaves things notoriously indeterminate as to whether impediments supplied by the market or private actors are to be considered violations of fundamental rights of citizens. By now, as interpreted, our tradition has recognized that the state must in some cases act to prevent private discrimination, but the whole terrain is contested, and the language of rights certainly does not resolve the difficulty.

Of course even libertarians believe that the state must act to secure rights—maintaining a system of contract, property rights, and so forth. Their list is a lot shorter than the list I favor, but they too believe that state action is required. Not even their state is purely negative. However, the libertarian position on the justifiability of state action and positive intervention is fluctuating and frequently unclear, whereas the CA makes it clear from the start that the state has an affirmative task of securing capabilities.

The Indian Constitution, by contrast to the US Constitution, typically specifies rights affirmatively.[32] For example: "All citizens shall have the right to freedom of speech and expression; to assemble peaceably and without arms; to form associations or unions; . . . [etc.]."[33] These locutions have usually been understood to imply that impediments supplied by nonstate actors may also be deemed violative of constitutional rights. Moreover, the constitution is quite explicit that affirmative action programs to aid the lower castes and

---

32. Not invariably: Article 14, closely modeled on the equal protection clause of the US Fourteenth Amendment, reads: "The State shall not deny to any person equality before the law or the equal protection of the laws within the territory of India."
33. Indian Constitution, Article 19.

women are not only not incompatible with constitutional guarantees but are actually in their spirit. Such an approach seems very important for gender justice. The state needs to take action if traditionally marginalized groups are to achieve full equality. Whether a nation has a written constitution or not, it should understand fundamental entitlements in this way.

The CA, we may now say, sides with the Indian Constitution and against the neoliberal interpretation of the US Constitution. It makes it clear that securing a right to someone requires more than the absence of negative state action. Measures such as the recent constitutional amendments in India that guarantee women one-third representation in the local *panchayats*, or village councils, are strongly suggested by the CA, which directs government to think from the start about what obstacles there are to full and effective empowerment for all citizens, and to devise measures that address these obstacles.

One place where Enlightenment notions of state inaction and negative liberty have been especially pernicious is in the state's relation to the household or family. The classic liberal distinction between the public and the private spheres aids the natural stand-offishness that many liberal thinkers have about state action. Even if it is fine for the state to act to secure people's rights, there is one privileged sphere in which they should not do this: the sphere of the family. Some liberal thinkers—for example, John Stuart Mill—have pointed out that nonintervention in the family allows egregious rights violations to go unaddressed: marital rape, domestic violence, child abuse. The notion of the "private domain" simply shields such abuses from scrutiny and correction.[34]

34. See Nussbaum 2000, ch. 4.

The language of capabilities does not automatically guarantee a critique of this baneful distinction. It all depends how one frames the capability list. If, however, one is in the habit of asking what each person is actually able to do and be, one will be very likely to notice that vulnerability to violence within the home stops women and children from doing and being many things they want to do and be, *and* have a right to do and be. More generally, asking about capabilities leads us to notice all sorts of inequalities women and girls suffer inside the family: inequalities in resources and opportunities, educational deprivations, the failure of work to be recognized as work, insults to bodily integrity. Feminists in the human rights domain have long been insisting that the notion of rights must be expanded to include women's rights to be free from abuse within the family, and they have achieved public recognition of women's rights against abuse in documents such as the Convention on the Elimination of All Forms of Discrimination against Women (CEDAW). Furthermore, the Declaration on Violence against Women, the appointment of the Special Rapporteur on Violence against Women, and the General Recommendations of the Committee on the Elimination of All Discriminations against Women have clarified that CEDAW does cover abuses that take place within the family. Nonetheless, the history and philosophical background of the notion of rights has made this a difficult struggle, given the traditional association of rights talk with the public-private distinction. Traditional rights talk neglected these issues, prior to the feminist critique of the past thirty years, and, even after CEDAW (which the United States, a nation with one of the highest rates of domestic violence, has never ratified), the feminist critique of rights continues to be contested. This is no accident. Rights language is strongly linked, historically at least, with the traditional distinction between a public sphere, which the state regulates, and a private sphere, which the state must leave alone.

CRITIQUE: FIRST AND SECOND GENERATIONS

Commonly, the human rights tradition has divided rights into two groups: the political and civil rights, which are often called first-generation rights, and the economic and social rights, which are called second-generation. This way of carving things up suggests that the political and civil rights have no economic and social preconditions. The CA has always insisted that they do. When we keep our eyes focused on what people are actually able to do and be, we quickly see that they do not have the ability to participate in political debate, to vote, to run for office, and so forth, if they are inhibited by extreme poverty, lack of education, and ill health—at least they do not have these entitlements securely, or on a basis of equality.

Thus the CA has insisted from the start that we refuse to make this misleading separation. All entitlements have material and institutional necessary conditions. Education, for example, is a distinct entitlement on its own, but it is also a precondition of the adequate exercise of a group of political rights. Domestic violence is bad *per se*, a violation of women's entitlement to bodily integrity. But it also impedes women from the exercise of many other capabilities, including the political capabilities.

By now some versions of the human rights approach would appear to grant the centrality of economic factors in securing the first-generation rights. But then the whole distinction ought to be dropped, and we should look at each entitlement separately, asking what its material and institutional preconditions are.

CONSEQUENTIALISM AND DEONTOLOGY

The family of human rights approaches looks distinctly deontological. It says that overall, good social consequences may not be pursued in ways that violate the items on the list of rights. Sen, however, has long argued convincingly that rights may be incorporated into an approach that focuses on producing overall good social consequences.[35] I agree with that analysis, although I would add the stipulation that the rights play a special role: they are entitlements for each and every person, and if they are violated, or not secured, there is a failure of basic justice, which cannot be adequately captured in the language of cost-benefit analysis.[36] There is thus a tragic aspect to a rights violation (to the failure to secure a central human capability) that distinguishes it from other failures to secure some social benefit.

Thus my version of the CA can be seen as a cousin of consequentialism, in the sense that it is what I call "outcome oriented." Whether the society is just is determined by looking at the outcomes it produces, including whether it secures the central capabilities to all citizens. It is in that way distinct from procedural approaches to justice that determine whether a situation is just by looking at the procedures that generated it.[37] It is, then, an outcome-oriented approach in which the securing of central capabilities plays a central role. Many human rights approaches have a similar structure, if they are developed as an overall account of political justice. Here, then, the CA seems to march in harmony with human rights approaches, even though it seems to be closer to consequentialism. As Sen has

35. Sen 1984.
36. Nussbaum 2001.
37. See Nussbaum 2005.

insisted, consequentialism need not be insensitive to the special importance of rights.[38]

There is one way, however, in which my CA, albeit a cousin of consequentialism, is not a form of consequentialism. Consequentialism is an overall view of the good and right. It says that the rightness of any choice is measured by whether it maximizes good consequences. I have argued, however, following John Rawls, that in a pluralistic society, containing many different religious and secular comprehensive views of the good, it is undesirable and disrespectful to base political choice on any comprehensive doctrine.[39] Instead, political principles should be only a *partial* view of the social good, and one that can, we hope, become the object of an *overlapping consensus* among the major religious and secular comprehensive doctrines. I have argued that my CA, and the capabilities list, can become the object of such a consensus.[40]

The reason why I use the term "outcome-oriented" rather than the term "consequentialist" to describe my approach is that I view consequentialism as a comprehensive ethical theory and thus not an acceptable source of political principles in a pluralistic society.

While we are on the topic of political liberalism, it may be time to clear up (again) a common misreading: *the CA is not a form of "cosmopolitanism."*[41] Although the approach includes an account of global as well as domestic justice, it would be a mistake to identify

38. Amartya Sen, "Rights and Capabilities," in *Resources, Values, and Development* (Oxford: Blackwell, 2004), 307–324. See also Sen 2004.

39. See John Rawls, *Political Liberalism*, expanded paperback edition (New York: Columbia University Press, 2006); Nussbaum 2000, 2005.

40. Nussbaum 2005.

41. Martha Nussbaum, "The Capabilities Approach and Ethical Cosmopolitanism: A Response to Noah Feldman," *The Pocket Part*, online supplement to *Yale Law Journal* (October 2007), http://yalelawjournal.org/the-yale-law-journal-pocket-part/international-law/the-capabilities-approach-and-ethical-cosmopolitanism:-a-response-to-noah-feldman/, accessed January 4, 2011.

it with the comprehensive ethical theory known as "cosmopolitanism," which is usually defined as the view that one's first loyalty should be to humanity as a whole rather than to one's nation, region, religion, or family. Cosmopolitans can probably accept most of what I recommend, but one does not have to be a cosmopolitan to accept the idea that all citizens (in one's nation, and then, in a second step, in all nations) should have a threshold amount of the ten capabilities. Most of the major comprehensive doctrines—religious and secular—can accept that idea, and few of them could accept a comprehensive cosmopolitanism. Whether my own comprehensive ethical doctrine is cosmopolitan or not is a separate questions (it is not, but it is close). The point that is relevant here is that the CA is a political doctrine. As such, it should not recommend any comprehensive ethical doctrine or be built upon one. Calling the CA a form of cosmopolitanism is tantamount to saying that it does not respect the diversity of religious and secular doctrines that all modern nations contain. But respecting that plurality is a central aim of my theoretical approach.

There is one criticism of the human rights idea that I wish to resist. That is the claim Sen once made that we should think of rights as part of a system of goals but not as having any power to "trump" the pursuit of social welfare.[42] I have argued against this claim in detail (Nussbaum 1997), and I will not repeat my arguments here. Suffice it to say that the central capabilities on my list, like human rights, are "trumps" in the sense that they have a very strong priority over the pursuit of welfare generally. If any one of them is not fulfilled, the nation is not even minimally just. Sen was arguing against Robert Nozick's account of property rights as "trumps" stopping redistribution of wealth and income in society. I agree with Sen that

42. Sen 1984.

Nozick's position is wrong, but I disagree about what is wrong with it. In my view, Nozick has the wrong account of property rights and ownership. We should not grant that people own what they happen to be holding on to: we should agree with Mill that, if some property is needed for the support of other people's basic entitlements, it is fine to take that property through taxation, and the person from whom it is allegedly taken did not even have just title to that property.[43] Both capabilities and rights, then, are "trumps," and I reject Sen's claim that capabilities are more soft or negotiable than rights—at any rate, not the central capabilities on my list.

WHAT ROLE FOR RIGHTS LANGUAGE?

If we have the language of capabilities, do we also need the language of rights? The argument in this chapter so far has defended the ongoing relevance and importance of the central concepts involved in the human rights tradition, since the CA is a species of the human rights approach. At this point, however, we still need to ask what the language of rights adds to the language of capabilities. Why should we continue to employ both, if we are convinced, as I am, that a version of the CA preserves what is best in the human rights tradition and avoids some deficiencies that some versions of that approach at times slip into?

We might want to be pragmatists here. The language of human rights has such wide currency and resonance in global politics that it would be rather unwise to try to do away with it—all the more since the CA is just a species of that approach, not a rival. But it would be good if we could say something more about why the language

43. See Nussbaum 1997.

of rights is independently useful and illuminating. I believe that we can.

The word "capability" does not by itself suggest the idea of an urgently important entitlement grounded in an idea of basic justice. The rest of my theoretical approach makes this point, by invoking ideas of human dignity, basic justice, a threshold amount of opportunity, and so forth. But the idea that capabilities are not just optional needs to be hammered home in any way we can, since people are all too inclined to think that we may deny people this or that important thing in order to pursue aggregate wealth. Indeed, when we note that the dominant approach in development economics still measures quality of life in terms of gross domestic product per capita, without asking whether these central individual entitlements have been secured, we can see why we should continue hammering.

Human rights language helps us perform that task.[44] When used as in the sentence "A has a right to have the basic political liberties secured to her by her government," the language of rights reminds us that people have justified and urgent claims to certain types of treatment, treatment that secures their central capabilities—no matter what the world around them has done about that. This is a key idea in my CA (although less clear in the more open-ended approach to entitlements mapped out by Sen).[45] So I can welcome the focus and intensification given to these key ideas by the language of human (and animal) rights.

By now, too, the human rights tradition has built up a wide array of valuable documents that describe central human entitlements in ways that have gained the support of the world community. Political action has mobilized around these documents, national

44. See also Sen 2004.
45. See Sen 1999.

constitutions have been written under their influence, and so forth.[46] We should not junk that tradition, we should instead make sure that it is connected to an analysis of what rights are; the CA supplies that analysis. When coupled with the idea of capabilities, as in the *Human Development Reports* of the United Nations Development Program, the idea of rights provides a valuable intensification, connecting the idea of capabilities to the ideas of social and political urgency and human centrality. The capabilities theorist or practitioner should not be skeptical of the language of rights but should employ it in close connection to the language of capabilities, thus making clear what analysis of rights is being offered.

The human rights tradition is a heroic struggle for basic justice. It would be foolhardy to turn away from that tradition. Nonetheless, the tradition has points of vagueness and unclarity. Here the CA can supplement it usefully. And it also has versions or offshoots that lead the mind away from important issues of justice. Here the CA supplies a valuable critique. The two approaches (one being a species of the other) should march forward as allies in the combat against an exclusive focus on economic growth, and for an approach to development that focuses on people's real needs and urgent entitlements.

46. See Sen 2004.

Chapter 4

Culture, Identity,
and Human Rights

KWAME ANTHONY APPIAH

Toward the end of September 1961, my father was thrown into prison in Ghana, on the orders of Dr. Kwame Nkrumah, president of our young republic. When the security police showed up—looking, so they said, for seditious documents—my mother asked them to search between every page of every book in the house. After a few hours they told her they were satisfied. "But you haven't finished," my mother said. "I want the president to be sure that my husband is innocent." She served them tea and sandwiches as they continued . . . she was, after all, an Englishwoman. We had a lot of books. By the end, they were begging her for permission to depart.

But they left the real challengers to the president behind. Because what buoyed up my parents in the face of my father's imprisonment and the threats of deportation against my mother wasn't *between* the pages of those books, it was *on* them. My father's beloved Romans, Cicero and Marcus Aurelius; my mother's United Nations of favorite poets, Matsuo Bashō, Okot p'Bitek, William Wordsworth, Léopold Sédar Senghor; the great nineteenth-century novels from Britain and France and Russia; modern American and African fiction; the King James Bible that my parents both loved so well.

Luckily, when my father and hundreds of others were arrested and imprisoned without trial, Amnesty International, the human rights NGO, had just been founded. Indeed, Amnesty's first fact-finding mission, in 1962, was to Ghana. And because this *was* the first Amnesty mission, my father was one of the first "prisoners of conscience."

Having your husband taken off to prison with no charges, no trial, and no date of release is, to state the obvious, a horrible experience. And if you have three young children (and a fourth on the way) and love has brought you to a foreign country with none of your own family nearby to rely on, it can be hard to keep the worry from reaching your kids. But I don't remember being too scared at the time. Because my mother—who was, I am proud to say, as extraordinary a person as my father—radiated confidence that our campaign to get our father out of jail would succeed. And that was in part because people in other countries sustained our family, people we did not know (people in Australia and Canada and India, people in other countries of Europe and Africa) who wrote because of Amnesty International to *our* president, to *their* newspapers, and to us to denounce the imprisonment of an innocent man.

When people are imprisoned without trial for speaking their minds, it is not a hard moral case: the perpetrators know that it's wrong and so does everybody else. And it's good to start with these clear cases. You see the wrong. You work with others to set it right. But the modern world is full of problems that are harder than that. And in facing those problems, those of us who want to make the world safer for people to lead lives of dignity have to do more than organize and act: we have to *think*. As a philosopher, that's my vocation, of course. I have the privilege of working in a global academic community full of people who study the many challenges in bringing closer a world of full human dignity.

So I am a deeply committed believer in the general thrust of the global regime of human rights to which the world committed itself when the UN General Assembly adopted the Universal Declaration of Human Rights on December 10, 1948, more than half a century ago. That language of human rights enabled the individual members of Amnesty International, as well the governments of many countries, to address the Ghanaian government on our behalf in language to which it was already committed. But, as I say, I am also deeply committed to a critical intellectual engagement with its ideas, its ideals.

And one thing that critical engagement reveals is that the meaning of the declaration depends upon a great wide world of human creativity: the poems and essays and novels, the movies and television dramas and stage plays, the painting and sculpture and music through which we learn—each of us and all of us together—to think about what matters to us, about the things that bring meaning and purpose to human life. The reason those books on my parents' shelves were enemies of what Nkrumah was doing—though they were friends of Nkrumah, the man, as they are of every human being—was that literature sustains and enriches the idea of human dignity, the idea in which the Declaration of Human Rights is grounded. As it says, in its first words,

> Whereas recognition of the inherent dignity and of the equal and inalienable rights of all members of the human family is the foundation of freedom, justice and peace in the world.

However, grasping the full meaning of those words requires a rich world of thought in the background, the whole realm of culture.

Now that word—*culture*—has had a hefty workout in recent years. Everyone now seems convinced that everything from anorexia to zydeco is illuminated by being displayed as the product of somebody's culture.[1] But *this* notion of culture is not the one I just relied on: the sense of culture in which we might concede that the determined operagoer is, as we say, "cultured." It's rather a different idea of culture—the anthropologist's idea—that each of us is enmeshed in socially transmitted meanings and practices: language, religion, cuisine; the practices that surround the central human transitions— birth, graduation, marriage, death; and, yes, literature and the arts as well, but only as a small portion of that vast assemblage.

It has become one of the most pious of the pieties of our age that we live in societies of enormous cultural diversity. And I don't want to deny either that diversity or our need to respond to it. But I do want to ask if it is really our *cultural* diversity, in this second, anthropological, sense that deserves attention.

And that's because the word "culture" is used here in yet a third sense to refer neither to socially transmitted practices and ideas nor to literature and the arts but to the groups that transmit them: the social groups that we also call cultures.

I have announced my topic as "culture, identity, and human rights," and I mean to discuss culture in these three senses and to say a little about the relationship of culture to human rights. But I think these three connected concepts have a variety of rather *different* significances for human rights. So I am going to propose a little preliminary terminological tidying up. When I'm discussing literature and the arts, I'm going to use the slightly old-fashioned

---

1. For anorexia, see Mervat Nasser, *Culture and Weight Consciousness* (New York: Routledge, 1997). For zydeco, see Dick Shurman, "New Orleans, Louisiana, and Zydeco," in *The New Blackwell Guide to Recorded Blues*, ed. John Cowley and Paul Oliver (Cambridge, MA: Blackwell Publishers, 1996).

word "civilization." I'll keep the word "culture" itself for the second sense: the sense in which anthropologists speak of the culture of Inuit or Ojibwe or Ulster Scots in Manitoba. And I'll use the words "identity" or "identity-group" to discuss culture in this third sense: the sense on which we speak of *a* culture, meaning a group—again like Inuit or Ojibwe or Ulster Scots.

So let's begin in a place where the idea of somebody's culture—in that anthropological sense—really does appear to explain something. And let me take the United States, which I know best, as my example (recognizing that there will be some important differences from the Canadian story). When Jews from the *shtetl* and Italians from the *villagio* arrived as immigrants at New York's Ellis Island, they brought with them a rich brew of what, in anthropologists' usage, we call culture. They brought a language and stories and songs and sayings. They transplanted a religion with specific rituals, beliefs, and traditions; a cuisine of a certain hearty peasant quality; and distinctive modes of dress. They came with particular ideas about family life. It was often reasonable for their new neighbors to ask what these first-generation immigrants were doing and why. A sensible answer would frequently have been, "It's an Italian thing"; "It's a Jewish thing": or simply, "It's their culture."

It is striking how much of this form of difference has gone from the United States. The proportion of foreign-born Americans is less than it was from 1860 to 1920; rates of exogamy among these older immigrant groups have soared just in the past few decades.[2] Fewer

2. Until 1960, less than 7 percent of Jews married out. Now it's more than half. http://www.jewishgentilecouples.com/resources/stats/33-marriagetrends.

Between 65 percent and 75 percent of Italian Americans now marry out. http://books.google.com/books?id=PGG6qUCO9S0C&pg=PA161&lpg=PA161&dq=italian+american+exogamy&source=bl&ots=nUkKd26JrB&sig=CjHsNyG4PeyGYN2dCToi159ImN0&hl=en&sa=X&ei=0xaAUr3mDdfZsASbzoKQAg&ved=0CCwQ6AEwAA#v=onepage&q=italian%20american%20exogamy&f=false.

and fewer Americans live in neighborhoods with a concentration of people who share their "national" origins. The rhetoric of diversity has risen as its demographic reality has declined.[3] There are still Seders and nuptial masses, still gefilte fish and spaghetti. But how much does an Italian name tell you, these days, about church attendance, or knowledge of Italian, or tastes in food or spouses, or attitudes to gay marriage? Even Jews, whose status as a small non-Christian group in an overwhelmingly Christian society might have been expected to keep their "difference" in focus, are getting harder to identify by a distinctive culture.

The immigration story doesn't apply, of course, to the descendants of African slaves, who have not had the privilege of becoming "white." Yet the striking contrast between black and white stories can lead us to neglect what they have in common. There are, indeed, forms of English speech that are recognized as black in America even if there are also large regional and class variations in black, as in white, speech. But what we are talking about here are all forms of *English*. Indeed, despite the vast waves of immigration of the last few decades, something like 97 percent of adult Americans—whatever their color—speak English "like a native"; with the occasional adjustment for an accent here and there, those 97 percent can all understand one other. Leave out recent immigrants and the number gets close to 100 percent.

Not only blacks and whites but also Asians and American Indians share the English language. Even Hispanics, the one American ethnic group *defined* by language, prove no exception. People talk a great deal about the Hispanization of America, and you can indeed hear Spanish spoken in stores and on street corners in places where you wouldn't have heard it forty years ago. But Hispanics in Florida

3. Mary Waters, *Ethnic Options* (Berkeley: University of California Press, 1990).

overwhelmingly believe that their children should speak English. In California, the vast majority of first-generation Hispanics have native fluency in English, and only half of their children speak Spanish at all.[4] If being American means understanding English, then US-born Hispanics overwhelmingly pass the test. Rates of English fluency run equally high among the children of immigrants from Africa and Asia.

Language is only one of many things most Americans share. My country is one, for example, where almost every citizen knows something about baseball and basketball and football. Americans shop American style and know a good deal about the same consumer goods: Coca-Cola, Nike, Levi-Strauss, Ford, Nissan, GE.

The supposedly persistent differences of religion, too, turn out to be shallower than you might think. In the main, American Judaism is, as is often observed, extraordinarily American. Catholics in my country are a nuisance for Rome just because they are . . . well, so Protestant. They typically claim individual freedom of conscience, for example—so they don't simply take the church's line on contraception or divorce or homosexuality.[5] Above all, most Americans who claim a religious affiliation (which now means 75 to 80 percent) regard it as essentially private, something for which they desire neither help nor hindrance from the government. Even parents who want prayer in the schools generally just want their own children sustained in their faith; they don't want the public school to set about converting the children of others. In these key respects—the sovereignty of the individual conscience within the

---

4. Geoffrey Nunberg, "Lingo Jingo: English Only and the New Nativism," *The American Prospect* 33 (July–August 1997), 40–47.

5. See Stephen Macedo, "Transformative Constitutionalism and the Case of Religion: Defending the Moderate Hegemony of Liberalism," *Political Theory* 26, no. 1 (February 1998), 56–89.

confession and the privacy of religious belief—American religion, whatever its formal sectarian designation, tends to be decidedly Protestant. Many of the religious traditions from Asia that have increased in significance in the present wave of immigration are also quickly Americanizing: much of American Islam, for example, is as happy with the separation of mosque and state as most Muslims elsewhere are resistant to it.

You might wonder if there isn't a connection between the thinning of the cultural content of identities and the rising stridency of associated minority rights claims. Those earlier European immigrants, with their richly distinct customs, were busy demanding the linguistic Americanization of their children, making sure they learned America's official culture. One suspects they didn't need to insist on the public recognition of *their* cultures of origin, because they simply took them for granted. Their middle-class descendants, whose domestic lives are conducted in English and extend eclectically from John Stewart to Chinese takeout, are discomfited by a sense that their identities are somehow *shallow* by comparison with those of their *nonnas* and *bubbehs*, and so they are busy demanding we all acknowledge the importance of their difference. And they call that difference "cultural diversity," even though, as I've been arguing, its cultural content in general—or its civilizational content in particular—is really quite modest.[6] Whatever marks American

6. Something similar has happened with African Americans. When there were still legal barriers to full citizenship, before the judicial decisions from *Brown v. the Board of Education* to *Loving v. Virginia* and the civil rights legislation of the 1960s, the public recognition of a unique black culture was not exactly the major item on the black political agenda. Black people wanted recognition by state and society of things they had in common with white people: their humanity and those famous "unalienable rights." In part as a result of these legal changes, middle-class African Americans, who were always quite close in language and religion to their white Protestant neighbors, are now in many cultural and economic respects even closer. And just at this moment, many of them have been attracted to an Afrocentrism that demands the recognition in public life of the cultural distinctness of

Jews or Catholics off from American Protestants, it isn't likely to be Jewish literature or Catholic music or Protestant poetry.

With these distinctions in mind—civilization, culture, identity— I want to turn now to thinking about the relationships between these three distinct, if interconnected, topics and issues about human rights.

Let's start with the third of these—identity—with the groups we call cultures and with their relation to human rights. One thing you often hear said about the Universal Declaration of Human Rights is that it is above all a charter of individual rights. Every one of us, the declaration asserts, each individual has inherent dignity; each individual one of us is born free and equal in dignity and rights; none of us—no individual—may be enslaved.[7]

African Americans: and mostly this means they seek recognition, in my terms, for a black civilization, for a black voice in literature and the arts.

I am not denying—who could?—that there are significant differences between the average experiences of blacks and whites in the United States. We all know of the concentration of the poorest blacks in inner cities with terrible schools and no jobs; the persistence of discrimination in housing, employment, and the legal system; and the tendency of whites to flee neighborhoods whose black populations rise beyond a "tipping point." Many poor urban blacks (like just as many poor rural whites) are doing badly in an economy that seems finally to be returning to doing well. All this I grant. But the fact is that the black middle class is also larger and doing better than it ever has; and it is largely they, not the poor, who have led the fight for the recognition of a distinctive African American cultural heritage— especially in the form of literature and the arts, black *civilization* in my terminology—just in a moment when cultural differences are diminishing.

7. This individual focus was thought to be a problem when the Organization of African Unity came to develop *its* charter of rights, so they called it the African Charter on Human and Peoples' Rights, in part to insist that Africans recognized that rights did not have to be individual. Though it's worth pointing out that the UDHR is not completely uncommunitarian: Article 29, Section 1, says, "Everyone has duties to the community in which alone the free and full development of his personality is possible."

In the decades since 1948, many people have come to the view that at least some animals have rights, too. And some—though fewer—believe that a range of other things, including plants and lakes and mountains, and perhaps nature or the earth, have rights we ought to respect as well. But unless you think human beings have no cause at all to give distinctive attention to the rights of human beings, it seems reasonable enough to have a Declaration of Human Rights and reasonable enough that it doesn't speak of the rights of other creatures.

And since human beings belong—as the UDHR recognizes—to national, religious, and other communities, and since the rights of these groups might reasonably be judged important human rights—but collective not individual ones—it would surely be wrong to ignore them (if, of course, there *are* any). The UDHR was developed in the shadow of genocide, and the idea of genocide presupposes that there is something especially wrong with seeking to erase an ethnic or racial group, a wrong beyond the murder of its members. Isn't this, one might ask, because the *group* has a *right* not to be treated in this way, not just because its members have that right individually?

One response to the threat of genocide is to seek a separate political fate, and one right that looms large in international politics is the right to self-determination, a right that could not coherently be articulated as an individual right. If the Palestinians—or, for that matter, the Quebecois—have a right to self-determination, it is one that they must exercise together, as a group. The declaration itself seems to assume that each people is entitled to democratic self-government.[8] That right too is something that cannot coherently be ascribed to individuals. Indeed, another famous declaration—the American Declaration of Independence—claims that "the People" have the right to "alter or to abolish" any government that is "destructive" of the end of securing the "unalienable rights" of its citizens, thus insisting on a group right to secure individual rights.

Whether articulated in the language of rights or not, protection for groups is especially important when they—like the indigenous peoples of the Americas or of Australasia—have suffered from a long history of oppression, a fact that is recognized in another UN

---

8. The language of Article 29, Section 2, appears to presuppose that we should all live in democratic societies.

General Assembly declaration, the one on the Rights of Indigenous Peoples (UNDRIP).[9]

The declaration does not explicitly mention the evils of sexism, racism, homophobia, xenophobia, and religious bigotry—the threats to groups that group rights sometimes seem to be aimed at answering. And these evils are not best met simply by insisting, as the declaration does, on equality of access to the fundamental rights regardless of "race, colour, sex, language, religion, political or other opinion, national or social origin, property, birth or other status." While this language certainly bars legal discrimination against individuals in virtue of these group memberships, you might look for a more explicit focus on protection for groups from the harms historically associated with these forms of status-based hostility or contempt—especially given the centrality of racism and homophobia in the Nazi regime whose destruction was the achievement of the Second World War.[10]

I am not saying that any of this requires a revision of the UDHR. Even if you believed in all the group rights I have canvassed, you could accept that the individual rights of human beings are more fundamental than any group rights and think that group rights,

---

9. http://www.un.org/esa/socdev/unpfii/documents/DRIPS_en.pdf.
10. The UDHR's list of protected statuses has other shortcomings. It does not explicitly acknowledge the existence of groups of people who need protection because of things they have done—criminals, migrants—or things that have happened to them—the disabled. Criminals gain recognition through their Article 10 and 11 due-process rights, but these are rights they share with those who are not guilty. After a fair trial on a criminal charge, however, you may become a prisoner. And prisoners, history suggests, face a particularly serious threat of rights' abuses, even if they are justly convicted.

Migrants, too, unlike settled ethnic minorities, often face the particular difficulty of securing their rights in a society whose culture and customs they do not fully comprehend. And the disabled face enormous difficulties beyond those imposed by their physical or mental condition as a result of the prejudices of the able-bodied. Finally there is aging, which is often associated with disability. The UDHR says nothing specifically about disability or aging and the aged, or about the rights of those who are dying or who wish to die.

where appropriate, are best articulated in separate documents like UNDRIP.

As for responses to racism and sexism, the UN system has now developed, through the UN Commission on the Status of Women and UNESCO's World Conferences against Racism, mechanisms for articulating a consensus on the wrongs done by these evils. The response to religious bigotry, especially in the form of Islamophobia, is, I believe, a genuine challenge for the international community. But I believe that recognizing a collective right against religious defamation, enforceable in international or domestic law, would actually make it harder to face up to this problem.[11]

For the disabled, we have the UN Convention on the Rights of Persons with Disabilities. Since 1955 the UN has had its Standard Minimum Rules for the Treatment of Prisoners, and in 2011 the UN commissioner for human rights issued a working paper on the rights of older persons. So, international human rights regime has responded on these issues despite their nontreatment in the UDHR.

And on the question of homophobia, there is a long way to go before we will reach a global consensus; still, progress has been swift in many places recently and the treatment of lesbian, gay, and y the UN commissioner for human rights has spoken of a "deeply disturbing pattern of violence and discriminatory laws and practices" affecting people on the basis of their sexual orientation and gender identity.[12] In sum, the issues of group rights some might see as

11. Kwame Anthony Appiah, "What's Wrong with Defamation of Religion?," in *The Content and Context of Hate Speech: Rethinking Regulation and Responses*, ed. Michael Herz and Peter Molnar (New York: Cambridge University Press, 2011), 164–182.

12. The European Court of Human Rights, in particular, has insisted that "sexual orientation is a concept covered by art 14," the anti-discrimination provision European Human Rights Convention. "The Court has held repeatedly," they reminded us in *Gas and Dubois v. France* in 2012, "that just like differences based on sex, differences based on sexual orientation require particularly serious reasons by way of justification." http://hudoc.echr.coe.int/

neglected in the UDHR have not always been ignored by the UN or the global human rights community.

In thinking about group identity and human rights, it may be helpful to introduce a distinction between *collective* rights, on the one hand, and *membership* rights, on the other.[13] Collective rights are rights that are exercised collectively. So, for example, the people of every nation have, as a matter of international law, the right to self-government. To make this collective right effective we have to be able both to identify a group and to define the mechanisms by which it can assert the right. Who are the Palestinians? Once we've identified them, we can grant them the collective right to self-government only through allowing them individually to participate in democratic procedures, which, if they are to be morally acceptable, must treat the individuals as equals with those outside the group. As a result, some individual rights seem to be implicated by the collective right to self-government. Nevertheless, self-government is something groups do. Individuals cannot do it, even though they can participate in it.[14]

sites/eng/pages/search.aspx?i=001-109572, para 59. For the comments of the UN commissioner for human rights see www.un.org/apps/news/story.asp?NewsID=46036.

13. See Anthony Appiah, *The Ethics of Identity* (Princeton, NJ: Princeton University Press, 2005), 72f.

14. Someone *might* argue, I suppose, that this is just a loose mode of speaking and that all the rights really involved here are individual. But that someone would need to say precisely how this claim should be unpacked. Even then, it is open to us to respond that the individual rights here exist because there is a collective right, and not the other way round. My thought is this: Someone might hold that citizens have the right to vote because they belong to a nation that has a collective right to self-government. The mechanisms by which a particular constitution allows individuals to participate in the exercise of that collective right may be normatively questionable. (Why, for example, can a majority of those voting, who may constitute a minority of those eligible to vote, determine what counts as the national will?) But the problems with the ways in which this idea is actually implemented don't, in themselves, show that we cannot proceed by deriving individual rights to vote from the collective right to self-government.

Membership rights, on the other hand, are individual rights that people have by virtue of their membership in groups. Voting rights are individual rights that we have as citizens, as members of a political people. The right to vote, once you reach the age of majority, in Manitoba elections is a membership right of Manitobans.[15]

You could say that only collective rights are genuine group rights, for only they involve assigning rights to groups. But I think that those who say they are skeptical about group rights often mean to be challenging membership rights.[16]

Still, it is worth insisting that there are many membership rights that are quite uncontroversial. Citizens, as I said, have voting rights *qua* citizens. It's not an objection to Canadian electoral laws that they don't grant citizens of Pakistan the vote. The vote is not the only such right, for Manitoba's Social Services Administration Act, for example, discusses grants "for the promotion, advancement, improvement, protection, or security, in any way, of the welfare of residents of the province."[17]

The sorts of group rights that have been introduced into law are often, as I have suggested, responses to evils like sexism, racism, homophobia, and religious bigotry. They are proposed so often because these harms affect all members of the group. Black people in

15. It is perhaps worth observing that laws barring discrimination against a group—say, women—grant membership rights to women, if they grant them a right of action when they are discriminated against as women, while laws barring discrimination on account of gender may not. But in a world of sexism, it would seem to me odd to favor the latter over the former on the grounds of hostility to group rights.

16. The laws of apartheid and Jim Crow assigned membership rights to whites (and membership disabilities to non-whites); some people have objected to them on that ground. But it seems to me that what was wrong was not so much that they assigned membership rights to whites but that they assigned them in a way that was intended to establish white supremacy. If the laws of apartheid had genuinely assigned rights to racial groups in ways that left them equal—or if Jim Crow laws had been genuinely "separate but equal"—they would have been objectionable, I think, but less so and for a different reason. Appiah 2005, 72f.

17. http://web2.gov.mb.ca/laws/statutes/ccsm/s165e.php. See 8(1).

the United States are treated in many public contexts as black. One such form of response is simple race prejudice. And the presence of significant numbers of US residents with anti-black prejudices, conscious and unconscious, combined with the fact that black people are in the minority, means that, on average, a black person enters most public contexts with a serious risk of paying higher psychic and material costs than otherwise identical white people. You are likely to get worse service, wait longer for it, and pay more for any goods whose prices are negotiable. You are more likely to be insulted or treated with contempt. Police officers are more likely to stop you and more likely to arrest you after stopping you. Prosecutors are likely to give you worse plea deals and ask for longer sentences. Juries are more likely to convict you and judges are likely to give you longer sentences than similarly accused whites. As a result of facts like these, you are more likely to be subjected to stress and to experience the ill health that flows from higher levels of cortisol and other physiological expressions of stress. Facts like these mean that the probability of race-based harms is generally higher for black people than for similarly placed whites.[18] That is why the United States has

18. This is one reason the bare fact of significant statistical differences in wealth and education by race would be important, even if it were not the result of racial animus. Because people cognitively store information (and misinformation) about race, the effect of these inequalities is to lead each black person, whatever her own place in the distribution, to be treated as presumptively less endowed with certain desirable attributes than the average white person. Such beliefs help to perpetuate, in obvious ways, the very inequalities they presuppose. And that adds to the race-based burdens facing black people. This is the basis for thinking that we might be able to establish the additional premise needed to get from the fact that it would be wrong to deny an individual a good just because she was black to the conclusion that the state is morally required to take affirmative measures to assure that black people *as a group* have roughly the same share of that good as other groups, other relevant things being equal.

You can be harmed directly by being denied a job or being physically assaulted. But you can also be harmed when the probability of your getting a job is lowered or the probability of your being assaulted is increased. Being black is associated in the United States with both direct harms and a multitude of probabilistic ones. While some lucky or well-off or

developed various forms of affirmative action, which involve membership rights for racial minorities. Affirmative action is based in the belief that, in some historical circumstances, you can best secure the individual human rights of members of a group by granting them collective rights—as when the Inuit in Canada are granted rights to manage their own territory—or membership rights—as when women are granted maternity leave.

On the other hand, there is no doubt that these forms of differential treatment can raise important challenges to the ideal of equality of rights that is also mentioned in the preamble to the UDHR. And one way of spelling out what that means is to say that a violation of one person's right weighs as much as the same violation of any other person's. So, provided that respecting collective and membership rights does not violate the *individual* rights of persons, there is no difficulty in granting equality in individual human rights to all, while securing these rights for groups as well.

But the ideal of equality requires more than this: it requires that in deciding which group rights to acknowledge we must not take sides, as it were, between identity groups. We must, to put it affirmatively, be neutral between them. I have argued before that in assessing the neutrality of a state act we should ask, "Would this person have been treated better had she been of some other identity?" Neutrality requires that the answer should be No.

In Canada in 2013 there was an instructive debate about this ideal of neutrality, a debate raised by the decision of the Québec

---

well-situated blacks can escape the direct harms, they cannot usually avoid the probabilistic ones. Taking special care may help them to avoid arrest, but they can do nothing to protect themselves from the fact that if they should be arrested, they would be more likely to be badly treated than similarly placed white people. Without attention to group differences like these you cannot assure that there will not be socially caused racial difference in life chances that wrong individuals.

government to offer a bill (Bill 60) that required that public servants in that province "maintain religious neutrality" and "exercise reserve with regard to expressing their religious beliefs" in the
course of their public duties. The duty of neutrality was interpreted
as specifically requiring them not to wear "objects such as headgear,
clothing, jewelry or other adornments which, by their conspicuous
nature, overtly indicate a religious affiliation" and to "exercise their
functions with their face uncovered, unless they have to cover their
face in particular because of their working conditions or because
of occupational or task-related requirements."[19] The law would also
have required people receiving services from public officials normally have their faces uncovered.

I confess that this law strikes me as misguided in a typically
French way: Similar laws in France against the veil and the burkha
(and the earlier laws in Turkey, inspired by the French legislation
Atta Turk admired) are just as erroneous. They interpret the notion
of state neutrality among religious identities in a way that is actively
hostile to specific religious groups, placing burdens on them that are
not placed on others. The fact that the law in question was tabled in
a legislature under the sign of a vast crucifix is surely revealing. That
it was not only rejected by the people of Québec but was partially
responsible for the electoral defeat of the government that proposed
it shows that many citizens grasped clearly what was wrong in these
proposals. Still, the problems with Bill 60 deserve spelling out.

Requiring people to be neutral among those they serve is, of
course, essential when they are acting for the state. I can also see the
case for "reserve" in the expression of religious beliefs since, generally speaking, public officials are not supposed to be discussing their

19. http://www.assnat.qc.ca/en/travaux-parlementaires/commissions/ci/mandats/Mandat-
24537/index.html.

religious beliefs in the course of their official duties. (Still, we might think reserve about all irrelevant matters is in order and not pick specially on religion.) But requiring people in the exercise of their office to conceal their religious identities imposes on them a burden that serves no obvious purpose. They are entitled, as a matter of right, to have religious views. They are not entitled to discriminate against people with other religious views. But what does what you wear have to do with whether you can discharge that duty? You may say that this is necessary in order to convince citizens receiving services that they are getting equal treatment. But surely only religious prejudice would lead a citizen to conclude she could not get fair treatment from a person of some identifiable religion. And if people of some religious affiliation really could not act neutrally, then the solution would be to deny them public employment, not to require them to conceal their religion.

The thought that a person wearing a kippah, or a foulard, or a visible crucifix somehow identifies the state with their religion would be plausible only if the state *required* it, not when the state merely *permits* it. The state does not endorse Paris fashion when a social security official shows up to work in one of Christian Dior's little black dresses. And, to repeat, if I really had reason to fear the non-neutrality of public officials of some religious affiliation, it is hard to see how my situation would be improved if that affiliation were made invisible to me.

The fact that the text of the draft law picked out one way of expressing religious identity—the veil—and banned it not merely for public officials but for citizens generally in their *dealing* with public officials makes it plain on its face that the law was addressed against Muslims. And the neutrality question—would we be legislating about this in this way if we were dealing with a Catholic practice?—answers itself firmly in the negative. Far from being an implementation, as was claimed, of neutrality, Québec's Bill 60 as proposed clearly violated it.

I have been exploring the relation between culture and rights in the sense of culture as identity: Québec's Bill 60 dealt with religious identity and got its significance for rights wrong. Let's turn now to culture in the anthropological sense and ask what its significance is for human rights. I shall return to the significance of civilization—literature and the arts—for human rights.

The American philosopher John Rawls, in *A Theory of Justice*, made a focus on fair distribution of what he called the "primary goods" a central concern of social justice. These primary goods, he wrote, "are things which it is supposed a rational man wants whatever else he wants." As "broad categories," Rawls cites "rights and liberties, opportunities and powers, income and wealth," but also "a sense of one's own worth."[20] This deliberately sketchy formulation appears to leave the door open to many other candidates—not least among them, as the Canadian philosopher Will Kymlicka says, being *culture*. "Rawls's own argument for the importance of liberty as a primary good is also an argument for the importance of cultural membership as a primary good," Kymlicka wrote in *Liberalism, Community, and Culture*. That's because autonomy requires choosing, and culture provides "the context of choice": it is "only through having a rich and secure cultural structure that people can become aware, in a vivid way, of the options available to them, and intelligently examine their value." Thus, the concern to shore up our culture "accords with, rather than conflicts with, the liberal concern for our ability and freedom to judge the value of our

---

20. "With more of these goods men can generally be assured of greater success in carrying out their intentions and in advancing their ends, whatever these ends may be." Thus, people in the original position know they want more rather than less of the primary goods. Rawls, *A Theory*, 92–93.

life-plans."[21] And Kymlicka's approach here is avowedly individual-ist, inasmuch as the good involved is ultimately a good to individu-als rather than groups. Hence his endorsement of what Iris Young calls "differentiated citizenship," the notion that "some forms of group difference can only be accommodated if their members have certain group-specific rights."[22]

Kymlicka has worked out, in commendable detail, a culture-friendly approach that aims to be consistent with the mainstream of liberal thought. His paradigm cases center on the aboriginal communities in Canada, to whom he would extend "cultural rights." (For example, these communities should be able to impose residency requirements, regulations as to land sale, etc.)[23] So these are collective rights. It might appear that the autonomy of the individual aboriginal is thereby sacrificed, at least to some degree, for the sake of the autonomy of the aboriginal group, but Kymlicka wants us to resist just this conclusion and see that, culture being a primary good, the autonomy of the individual depends upon the sustenance of the "societal culture" to which he or she belongs.

21. Kymlicka, *Liberalism, Community, and Culture* (Oxford: Oxford University Press, 1991), TK. Or, in a later formulation: "Put simply, freedom involves making choices amongst vari-ous options, and our societal culture not only provides these options, but also makes them meaningful to us." Kymlicka, *Multicultural Citizenship*, 83.

22. Kymlicka, *Multicultural Citizenship*, 26; Iris Marion Young, *Inclusion and Democracy* (New York: Oxford University Press, 2000).

23. He further observes, "A recent United Nations report rejected the view that Article 27 is nothing but a nondiscrimination provision: it insisted that special measures for minority cultures . . . are required and that such measures are as important as nondiscrimination in defending fundamental human rights in this area. . . . They also may involve the recognition that minority cultures are entitled to protect themselves by placing limits on the incursion of outsiders and limits on their own members' choices about career, family, lifestyle, and exit." Jeremy Waldron, "Minority Rights and the Cosmopolitan Alternative," *University of Michigan Journal of Law Reform*, Vol. 25 (1992) 758.

Charles Taylor, the other leading Canadian philosopher of multiculturalism, thinks the argument for cultural rights is not just a matter of getting individuals what they are entitled to. "As individuals we value certain things; we find certain fulfillments good, certain experiences satisfying, certain outcomes positive," he concedes. "But these things can only be good in that certain way, or satisfying after their particular fashion, because of the background understanding developed in our culture." A conclusion follows swiftly: "If these things are goods, then other things being equal so is the culture that makes them possible. If I want to maximize these goods, then I must want to preserve and strengthen this culture."[24]

There is much to be said about these approaches. But the practical challenge of the idea of a group's right to culture is to try and figure out what duties it imposes on those outside the cultural group. We might construe the right to culture negatively as a right against suppression. You—the you here is anyone, but especially governments, which may have the power to do these things—you may not interfere with what we might all a person's exercise of her culture: the language, the practices of everyday life, the religious traditions she has inherited from the social group to which she belongs. You may not ban a language, suppress religious practices, stop people dancing their dances, singing their songs, telling their tales; you may not ban their marriage ceremonies, their first communions, their Seders, their Haj's, their funerals. Or rather, you may not do so without a very good reason. People are presumptively entitled to live in these ways, should they choose to. But if it turns out that the religious practices cause harm to their children or endanger the health of the community, then we may intervene—not because we

24. Taylor, "Irreducibly Social Goods," in his *Philosophical Arguments*, 136.

disapprove of the practices and the ideas themselves but because they have harmful effects.

We could construe the right to culture more affirmatively. Not only must you not get in the way, you must actively assist the group if it needs help in keeping up its language and traditions. Maybe, for example, they can't afford the teachers who will keep their children literate in their language. Then we should make sure such teachers are available to them in the public schools or through their community centers. Perhaps they are an immigrant community that needs help bringing in a religious teacher from their country of origin.

But whichever way you construe the right to culture—whatever obligations you think it places upon the government—you will have to ask questions like these. Who gets to decide which version of the culture is to be sustained? If the men tell us, for example, that the tradition is one in which women have no political authority, does that mean we should allow all requests to be channeled through the men? What happens if the women tell us they want something else? Or, that they would like to see the culture change?

The point is that once the government is in the culture business it has to respect the fundamental ideas of neutrality that I have already insisted on: the idea that people matter irrespective of their identities. If the people of a social group have practices they want to sustain, and those practices are not morally offensive, then so be it. But taking sides in the disputes within groups about what is and what is not worth sustaining is usually going to involve taking sides between women and men, or young and old, or traditionalists and modernizers. And that will usually violate the government's duty of neutrality.

The worry about the right to culture is not, let's be clear, a worry about people's having some culture or other. No human being who is normally raised in a normal society will reach maturity without some language, without some practices that she understands, without some sense of right and wrong, or without some notions about what is worthwhile in human life. These are all products of her instincts and her experiences. To say that everyone is entitled to *this* is only to say that they are entitled to be socialized, given an education, prepared for life. But people who talk about a right to culture are concerned that Jews have a right to Jewish culture, the Irish a right to Irish culture, and so on. The worry is not about having some culture or other; it is about sustaining a culture that is theirs. And the right way to respond to this is not to require Jews to be Jewish or Catholics to be Catholic or Muslims to be Muslim, of course: It is to make sure that we don't get in the way of their living a Jewish or Catholic of Muslim life if they so choose. And that means that we must also allow those in their communities who *don't* want to live a Jewish or Catholic or Muslim life to be free from illegitimate forms of constraint by their communities. We cannot require observant Jews to be nice to those who wish to lead un-Jewish lives, and so mutatis mutandis for the other cases. But we should certainly stop them interfering with others' liberties, if they tried to; this, however, is only the application of the idea that the government should secure the liberties of its citizens, including protecting us from each other.

Let me turn now, briefly, in closing, to the question of civilization and human rights. Article 27, Section 1, of the UDHR says, "everyone has the right freely to participate in the cultural life of the community." It then immediately glosses this as a right "to enjoy the arts and to share in scientific advancement and its benefits," which makes it plain that what the declaration has in mind is a right to participate in what I am calling civilization. Unfortunately, as you see, the UDHR's language suggests that you only have a right to access the civilization of your own community. This strikes me as quite wrong. The civilization people should have free access to is any civilization that engages them. And the most important human right here, in the sense of the declaration, is the right to education of Article 26—an individual right, to be sure, but one that can only be exercised in a community.

For through education we gain access to civilization. We learn to read poetry and the novel, to understand science and music, to appreciate painting and sculpture. And if we learn to value these things we will immediately be led away from a parochial understanding of them. Shakespeare was inspired by Petrarch's Italian sonnets and Livy's stories from Greece and Rome. One of Goethe's great poetry cycles is called the West-Östliche Divan—the latter being, of course, a Persian word—because it was inspired by the fourteenth-century Persian poet Hafez (whose tomb is still a place of cultural pilgrimage for Iranians). There are reasons for resisting the idea that culture, or at any rate the stuff we rightly care about most, is national in any deep sense—or that it matters to us only through our particular identities.

Civilization—the life of science, literature, and the arts—is sustained in part by our individual human rights: the right of free expression, freedom of religion, and the right to education. All of these help to make a living civilization possible. And conversely, as I said at the start, the great monuments of civilization help us to understand what is worth doing in human life and thus empower us to live the lives of dignity that the whole regime of human rights is meant to make possible. Without this rich world of civilization human rights would be endangered. People would not understand *why* we are entitled to the forms of respect that underlie protection of our rights.

Here, so it seems to me, we are in territory that was already marked out by the UDHR, which said that its aim was to proclaim

> this Universal Declaration of Human Rights as a common standard of achievement for all peoples and all nations, to the end that every individual and every organ of society, keeping this Declaration constantly in mind, shall strive by teaching and education to promote respect for these rights and freedoms and by progressive measures, national and international, to secure their universal and effective recognition and observance.

So, one aim of the declaration was precisely to make sure that the culture and civilization of people of every identity would help sustain our human rights. But though civilization is grounded in particular societies and identities it is not the sole possession of the nations and peoples whose members created it. And we are more likely to respect the human rights of all peoples if we live in a world of fruitful, ongoing exchange of civilizations.

These are the ideals of cosmopolitanism. We should recognize the human rights of all, at the same time respecting their different cultures and learning from their diverse civilizational accomplishments. Only in reaching beyond our identities do we fully find ourselves. It is a message to be found over and over again in literature and the arts, as when Georges Braque, inventor with Picasso of Cubism, said: "Les masques nègres m'ont ouvert de nouveau horizons. Ils m'ont permis d'entrer en contact avec l'instinctif, opposition à cette fausse tradition qui veut que l'on repousse ce qui fait peur."[25] *African masks opened new horizons for me. They allowed me to*

25. http://fr.wikipedia.org/wiki/Georges_Braque#cite_note-Jean_31-22.

enter into contact with the instinctive, in opposition to that false tradition that wants us to reject what makes us afraid. Or—and let me close with these words—when W. B. Yeats writes about Rabindranath Tagore: "A whole people, a whole civilization, immeasurably strange to us, seems to have been taken up into this imagination; and yet we are not moved because of its strangeness, but because we have met our own image, as though we had walked in Rossetti's willow wood, or heard, perhaps for the first time in literature, our voice as in a dream."[26]

26. W. B. Yeats, "Introduction" to Rabindranath Tagore, Gitanjali (London: Macmillan and Co., 2013), 7.

Chapter 5

Indigenous Love, Law, and Land in Canada's Constitution

JOHN BORROWS

IN THE BEGINNING ... MEWINZA AABIDING

I begin with a story; it's a love story.[1] It's an old story. It's a story about devotion and loss. Innocence, lust, greed, and betrayal appear in full measure. The setting is hauntingly beautiful, and precarious. We're on the windswept shores of a stone-grey lake. Ice gathers at its limestone edges. Snows spirals from nearby cedars. Ancient escarpments, etched with heavy frost, tower over distant tree lines.

The plot is complicated, but its main lines are clear: Paradise, lost. A promised land, and cruel exile. Milton's language could serve as prologue:

> For how shall I relate
> To human sense the invisible exploits

1. I would like to thank the following individuals for their helpful comments on earlier drafts of this article, including Hannah Askew, Benjamin Berger, Jean Borrows, Jennifer Borrows, Joseph Borrows, Lindsay Borrows, Robert Gibbs, Jeff Hewitt, Aaron Mills, Heidi Stark, Jason Stark, Jim Tully, and Emily Snyder.

Of warring Spirits? how, without remorse,
The ruin of so many.[2]

The Anishinaabe trickster, Nanaboozhoo, is on the scene. Jesus and Sir John A. MacDonald also make appearances. The queen wears a nice hat. The cast of characters is broad. Most are nameless. Simple farmers, woodsmen, and city folk perform alongside hunters, fishers, and Indian chiefs.

Looking closer, our gaze sharpens. A faraway sign comes into focus. We struggle toward it, though it's periodically obscured by flurries. The snows are knee deep. Each step pushes us through the crust. Soon we are breathing heavily. Our hearts pound in our ears. We notice frail, tendril hands rising from the frozen expanse. They resist internment, silently grasping at the white swarm. Mute, and shorn of their flesh, they are weak. Yet they climb in crippled splendor—last season's skeletons fighting from their graves. It's the old plants: Queen's Anne lace, timothy grass, chokecherry bushes, and milkweed stalks. They stab through the snow, resisting burial in the gathering storm.

As we walk, slowly, our efforts pay off. We finally draw close to the sign: Neyaashiingmiing. It's the Cape Croker Indian Reserve, on Georgian Bay. Seeing the sign, at the water's edge, creation comes into view. A giant turtle rises from the depths. The world is born and then we witness the fall: It has something to do with apples and strawberries. Then we're in the lone and dreary world. We realize we are cast out of our homelands. We search for atonement. We long for reconciliation, though all we feel is the harsh storm.

2. John Milton, *Paradise Lost and Other Poems* (New York: Mentor Books, 1961), bk. 5, lines 564–568.

But we remember that this is a love story, and then we are confused. What we love has been lost. It's been stolen, fair and square, with kindness, deceit, and trickster-like efficiency.

Our sign stands at a river mouth: zaagiin. Beneath the crust we know its power flows, even in this season.

Thus, our story unfolds. Our protagonists, hearing waters underfoot, search for ways to rescue their love from the cold Canadian winter.

This chapter asks whether love has any place in the language of rights in Canada. Section 35(1) of the constitution states, "The existing Aboriginal and treaty rights of the Aboriginal peoples of Canada are hereby recognized and affirmed." I argue that this provision, alongside indigenous peoples' own legal traditions, creates a space for love in Canada's highest laws.

The following chapter unfolds in four parts. First, I discuss love's relevance in public life. Second, I explain how Canadian law incorporates indigenous laws related to love into its framework. Third, I consider how Anishinaabe law characterizes love. Finally, I apply Anishinaabe principles related to love to show how indigenous rights over reserves and traditional territories would fare if we more consistently applied the Supreme Court's constitutional framework about the relevance of indigenous law in Canada.

Love, Law, and Politics: Love's Relevance in Public Life

My family has always admired Louis Riel, the Metis leader.[3] One reason may be that my great-great-great-grandmother was a Riel.[4]

---

3. An excellent biography of Louis Riel is Joseph Boyden, *Louis Riel and Gabriel Dumont* (Toronto: Penguin, 2010).
4. My great-great-great-grandmother's name was Therese. She was from a Metis fur-trading family around Sault St. Marie, though we are not sure if she was Louis's blood relation. Her daughter eventually moved south and east to marry an Anishinaabe man. They passed their

We have long recognized Louis Riel's complexities but nevertheless held his name in the highest esteem. He tried to love and serve his people along with others who moved among them. He expressed these sentiments in a prayer he penned when he decided not to become a priest. In a letter to Archbishop Tache, on January 8, 1876, Riel spoke about serving society out of love. He wrote, "I love the world; I want to pass my life there . . . I beg You, give me as a layman the circumstances, the opportunity and Your help so that through-out my life, even to the last breath I earn You more glory . . . I work more effectively for the good of society."[5] The spirit of Riel's words, love's relevance to public life, is at the heart of this chapter.

In contemporary Canada, political and legal language seem generally devoid of references to love. We inhabit public spaces which are putatively neutral. They seem designed to hide feelings. Thus our statutes, cases, and regulations are filled with technocratic legalese and bureaucratic jargon. Furthermore, love is not regularly regarded as a necessary practice among political allies. It is certainly not encouraged among political adversaries. This is even or per-haps particularly the case in relation to indigenous issues. Thus, for most people, it would be the height of folly to view love as a realistic benchmark for law and political agreement. It could be seen as chill-ingly and childishly naive.

Despite this truth, love is a familiar ideal in other spheres of life. Family relationships generally strive to place love at their heart.

lives on the south shores of Lake Huron, in Anishinaabe communities in close proximity to Metis communities at Southampton, Owen Sound, and Penetanguishine. For a history of these relationships, see Patsy Lou Wilson McArthur, ed., *Historic Saugeen and Its Metis People* (Belleville, ON: Epic Press, 2005). For a discussion of the legal implications found within family histories in this area, see John Borrows, "A Genealogy of Law: Inherent Sovereignty and First Nations Self-Government," *Osgoode Hall Law Journal* 30 (1992), 291.

5. Tom Flanagan, *Louis "David" Riel: "Prophet of the New World"* (Toronto: University of Toronto Press, 1979), 36.

Without love, a parent-child or marriage relationship falls short of our fondest dreams. Love is a key to most spiritual and religious practices. Love is a prominent part of our friendships. It is found in our formative teaching relationships. We see it in primary school and through to university. Love and its absence is a constant subject of artist expression. Song, poetry, writing, movies, and other media weave it through every human endeavor. Love is at the center of our own sense of worth. It forms a strong part of our desires to reach out and work with others.

So why is love not an explicit political or legal standard or aspiration, particularly when we think about rights?[6]

Despite conflicting examples, I expect love is a motivating force in the lives of many legislators in Canada. Public service is an obvious venue for advancing or protecting some group, cause, or locale that is near the center of one's care and concern. Of course, we must be as quick to acknowledge other factors are in play. Greed, ambition, self-aggrandizement, dislike, or animosity toward others are also political motivators. These powerful forces seem to demonstrably outweigh any sentiment like love in day-to-day parliamentary, legislative, or judicial affairs.

Nevertheless, most would likely concede that love is a factor in political life, even if it is not the dominant value. Though partisans would disagree, we do not generally elect monsters to political office in Canada. The legislation they draft is often motivated by the best of intentions, though we may hate their sentiments. If most of us were in their shoes we might admit that love of God, family, country,

---

6. For discussions of how love informally and implicitly is woven into law and politics, see Paul Kahn, *Law and Love: The Trials of King Lear* (New Haven, CT: Yale University Press, 2000); Martha Nussbaum, *Love's Knowledge: Essays on Philosophy and Literature* (New York: Oxford University Press, 1992); Elizabeth Povinelli, *The Empire of Love: Toward a Theory of Intimacy, Genealogy and Carnality* (Durham and London: Duke University Press, 2006).

the environment, or some other cause would motivate our service. While we might delude ourselves in such a self-evaluation, because our motivations are really more prosaic, the point remains. Love is an important internal self-explanation for many public-spirited actions.

So, I ask the question again: Why are concepts of love absent in legal language and debate?

I can think of at least three initial objections to its inclusion. First, perhaps love is not applied to our legal processes because law is regarded as coercive. Law may be enacted through love, but we can never require people to love one another. Love cannot be forced.[7] It is only meaningful if it is free from compulsion and domination. Secondly, the concept of love can be remarkably vague and ambiguous. It has many meanings. If legally relevant, it would create conflicting claims about what adherence to its precepts would require in particular situations. Since appeals to love would generate apparently contradictory results, its currency is probably undervalued. It does not produce certainty or cultivate efficiency in our broadest public sphere. As part of these definitional concerns, perhaps love is

---

7. Love cannot be forced, at least among humans. For arguments that love can be commanded by God, see Franz Rosenzweig, *The Star of Redemption* (Madison: University of Wisconsin Press, 2005), 190:

Can love then be commanded? Is not love fate and being gripped, and if still free, then only as a free gift? And now it will be commanded?

Yes, indeed. Love cannot be commanded, no third can command or compel it. No third can, but the One. The command of love can come only from the mouth of the lover. Only the lover, but he actually can speak and does say: Love me. In his mouth this command of love is no strange command, rather *it is nothing but the voice of love itself.* The love of the lover has really no other word to express itself except the command.

. . . But the imperative command, the immediate, arisen in an instant, and in the instant of its arising also already sounding—because *in the imperative arising and sounding are one*—The "Love me!" of the lover is wholly perfected expression, wholly pure speech of love.

so closely associated with intimacy that we reject its application in so-called public life. Even though political and legal relations can be very personal and affect the intimate details of our lives, there may be a tendency to reserve its use for relationships with those we do not consider to be strangers. Third, references to love may also be excised from political life because employing them may be regarded as cheapening and degrading the concept, reducing love to a meaningless slogan or mindless refrain. No one wants to hear public servants talk about love in vacuous, empty, or self-serving terms.

I agree with the gist of these critiques: In politics, love cannot be forced, it can be too abstract, and appeals to its power can be abused. While these points are all true, they do not tell the complete story. There are excellent reasons to be wary of love's appearance in the law, but we should not exile the concept from public life. Rather, it should be understood in more nuanced terms. Love is part of political affairs, even if we have not paid it much attention. Thus, we must engage in a more fine-grained analysis. Simple binaries, dichotomies, and either-or categories are insufficiently rich in considering this issue. The general weight of our objections can stand, even as we acknowledge other dimensions of these arguments which recognize love's place in law and public affairs.

First, as argued above, love as a legal and political concept should be rejected if its invocation diminishes others' agency. Appeals to love which are patriarchal, patronizing, and infantilizing should never be an acceptable part of legal or political life. Languages of love must be decolonized.[8] They must reject gendered and racialized dimensions which disempower women and adversely discriminate on the basis of

8. Dawn Rae Davis, "(Love Is) the Ability of Not Knowing: Feminist Experience of the Impossible in Ethical Singularity," *Hypathia* 17 (2002), 146. Love is a problem for feminist postcolonial theory and philosophy precisely because the discourses of love and benevolence were used to disguise imperialism's violence.

any other right and freedom. Love should not stand first, or alone, in any political and legal lexicon. It should not be problematically prioritized. Love must always be integrated with protections and practices found more broadly in our systems. I do not claim that love lies at law's foundation. In fact, I reject foundational, universalized, idealized, or essentialized appeals to love. Calls to love can be co-opted and abused to serve narrow, selfish, and discriminatory purposes; they can be very destructive. Lawyers, judges, politicians, and others might argue that *their* way of loving is foundational and therefore coerce others to purposes they do not share. The Indian Act, residential schools, and the theft of indigenous lands remind us of love's bitter fruits. The language of love can be dangerous, and we must be exceedingly wary of its appearance. It can be domineering, sadistic, and subordinating.

At the same time, we should not reject love out of hand. It can be an important aspect of law and public affairs if it is checked and counterbalanced by other concerns. Love can be exercised in ways which incorporate other values, rights, and freedoms. Thus, while I assert that love is extraordinarily important in legal and political affairs, I do not claim that it should be universally determinative in any sphere. Appeals to love must always be contextual; they must be rigorously scrutinized and intensely critiqued. Appeals to love must be precisely calibrated to each situation under review to ensure its application is liberating and enhances agency. My point is that love must always be regarded as only provisionally relevant to the law. To be clear, I am also advancing a contrasting point: love can and should often be irrelevant to law. We must reject sweeping calls for both the relevance and the irrelevance of love to the law; either claim can be deployed for coercive purposes.[9]

9. Since I do not start from any preexisting philosophical or legal position about love's all-embracing relevance to the law, I would build a case for its relevance by reference to other

Furthermore, in acknowledging that love should never be forced, it is also important to admit that coercion is only one dimension of the law. Many laws flowing from our political processes are designed to enhance freedom, autonomy, and choice. Laws can incentivize choice; as such they promote the pursuit of diverse and even contradictory goals. People are encouraged to develop their own interests, resources, and diverse goals through law. Our constitutional system attempts to facilitate freer formation of contracts, more productive uses of land, and the creation of meaningful social bonds. Our statute books are filled with provisions which place autonomy rather than coercion at the heart of their purposes. Thus, it is possible to contemplate that love might be legally relevant, as persuasion stands alongside coercion in our law.

Thus, in considering love's legal relevance, we must remember that law also rests on persuasion. Political parties attempt to persuade voters of the attractiveness of their policies or ideological orientation when they campaign for office. If they fail in this task, they may not be elected. The formation of these alliances requires at least some plausible explanations and justifications in garnering support. Moreover, persuasion is also evident when disputes arise about the application of laws passed by governments. Judges engage in deep discussions with affected parties' representatives to provide detailed reasons for upholding or striking down a law. While coercion is definitely part of our legal world, these examples demonstrate it has other dimensions. Love should not be erased from our legal and

correlative and contrasting values, like equality, freedom of speech, freedom of assembly, etc. I would be very hesitant to make love the sole value for legal change in any circumstances. At the same time, I am arguing that love should be available as one of our standards for legal and political judgment, when it can persuasively be shown to be consistent with the other rights and freedoms found within Canada's constitution. For further discussion about a nonfoundational view of law and politics, see John Borrows, *Freedom and Indigenous Constitutionalism* (Toronto: University of Toronto Press, 2015).

political vocabulary just because aspects of our system are coercive. Law is not just about force—it also requires our participation and agreement.

Second, in considering love's definitional ambiguity, we might ask why concepts like life, liberty, security, equality, freedom, peace, order, and good government are present in our legal lexicon. They are equally complex, vague, and abstruse. These principles can also be used to subordinate, colonize, and dominate others. Like love, their invocation has been and can be extremely dangerous for those who are vulnerable to abuses of power in our society. Many have been oppressed through appeals to equality, liberty, and security. Despite their misuse, these concepts are political talismans; they lie at the center of our constitutional commitments. We have no difficulty expecting the state to abide by these principles. Ambiguity is a legal reality in all rights language. Rights are necessarily expressed in general terms to provide wide-ranging protections against state intrusions. Their broad framing has not prevented us from giving them meaning in particular cases. So, while rights like life and equality are vague and ambiguous, most Western legal systems have developed standards and tests to give them real force in individual and institutional terms. While ideas like security and peace do not have precise definitions, they nevertheless play a role in protecting individuals from harm. Despite their generality, they also facilitate government action in aiding those who are oppressed in society. Thus, concepts of life, liberty, security, equality, peace, order, and goodness are not cheapened by their inclusion as rights in Canada's constitution. If anything, their very breadth elevates our expectations. It heightens the public demand we place on these concepts. Love can stand alongside these ideas and enhance our public life.

We also had a third concern: about love being an improper legal source because of its connection to intimacy. Discussions about intimacy should cause us to probe customary law. Not all Canadian law emanates from legislative or judicial chambers.[10] In fact, most law in Canada rests on customary norms and practices. Custom can be more implicitly a place of love. Most of us participate in patterns of behavior that do not require the police or any formal authority to ensure peace, order, and good government. We respect the life, liberty, security, and equality of others because of customary law's intimate, subtle, informal force.[11] Customary laws are inductive. We imply the obligations they produce through societal contexts.[12] Without customary law, formal law as it emerges from legislatures and courts would not take us very far. Many countries have outstanding statutes and well-reasoned judicial opinions, yet life is degraded because customs which reinforce love are absent in public life. The great American jurist Oliver Wendell Holmes once observed, "The life of the law has not been logic, it has been experience."[13] We would not likely have effective laws in Canada without

10. Roderick MacDonald, "Custom Made: For a Non-chirographic Critical Legal Pluralism," *Canadian Journal of Law and Society* 26 (2011), 301. For more general literature decentering the role of positivistic law, see Robert Ellickson, *Order without Law: How Neighbors Settle Disputes* (Cambridge, MA: Harvard University Press, 1991); Eric Posner, *Social Norms, Nonlegal Sanctions, and the Law* (Northampton, MA: Edward Elgar, 2007); Austin Serat and Thomas Kearns, eds., *Law in Everyday Life* (Lansing: Michigan State University Press, 2009); Jean Braucher, John Kidwell, and William C Whitford, eds., *Revisiting the Contracts Scholarship of Stewart Macaulay: On the Empirical and the Lyrical* (Oxford: Hart Publishing, 2013).

11. General definitions of customary law can be found in J. Brierly, *The Law of Nations*, 4th ed. (Oxford: Clarendon Press, 1949), 60; *Black's Law Dictionary*, 6th ed. (St. Paul, MN: West Publishing, 1990), 384.

12. Gerald Postema, "Implicit Law," in *Rediscovering Fuller: Essays on Implicit Law and Institutional Design*, ed. Willem Witteveen and Wibren Van der Burg (Amsterdam: Amsterdam University Press, 1999), 255.

13. Oliver Wendell Holmes Jr., *The Common Law* (Boston: Little, Brown, 1881), 1.

these more democratic, intimate, customarily lived roots. Love easily entwines itself into this sphere. I would argue this is the heart of Canada's constitutional system of rights and freedoms. Most of us are expert legal practitioners in the field of customary law. We generally respect the autonomy and liberty of our neighbours through countless redistributive and restraining acts.

Even though I am cautious, I hope you can see why I suggest that love should play a more explicit role in understanding, protecting, and advancing rights within Canada's constitutional structure. It already has a role in the law, could be given meaning in particular contexts, and can be part of law's persuasive power.

Before I proceed apply this insight to aboriginal and treaty rights, however, there is one more issue I wish to address. It is that we must recognize and create legal spaces for enmity, opposition, and even hatred to be played out in our society, even as we simultaneously allow and expect love to be a more persuasive force.

One of the greatest insights in political philosophy was voiced by Thomas Hobbes. He concluded that political life was nasty, brutish, and short.[14] He doubted that society would ever coalesce through law on its own accord. In fact, Hobbes felt that societal-wide political consensus was impossible. He lived through the bloody English civil war. He saw how people disagreed about the fundamental purposes of life and political organization; he knew they did not see eye-to-eye in how they should govern themselves. Since societies had too little common ground to forge healthy relationships, Hobbes proposed a concept of government which could accommodate disagreement, opposition, and animosity. We are heirs to that proposal. He distinguished political from civil society. He proposed

---

14. Thomas Hobbes, *Hobbes: Leviathan: Revised Student Edition* (Cambridge: Cambridge University Press, 1996), 89.

a "leviathan" to govern us in the political sphere, to permit freedom in the civil sphere.[15] He believed coercive sovereignty was necessary to bring people of differing views into political relationships. While I disagree with the emphasis Hobbes gives to disagreement in public affairs and his public/private distinction, I believe his insight about disagreement must be heeded for effective constitutional governance. We must design systems of government which reinforce and accommodate deeply differing and contrasting points of view, even as we strive for greater consensus in many spheres.[16]

Government must be built out of and include our disagreements, as well as attending to agreement, unanimity, and accord. Thus, while I argue that love should have a more prominent place in framing our rights, freedoms, and governance in Canada, I also strongly believe that opposing manifestations must be recognized, affirmed, and accommodated within our structures and practices. Nothing in this chapter should ignore this fact. As noted, I am not making an argument for the primary virtue of love as a political and legal value.[17] I do not want to universalize or essentialize its definition and application. I do not regard any legal or political right or value, including love, as foundational to Canada's constitutional

15. For a critique of public/private distinctions in the law, see Duncan Kennedy, "Stages of the Decline of the Public/Private Distinction," *University of Pennsylvania Law Review* 130 (1081), 1349; Jeff Weintraub and Krishan Kumar, eds., *Public and Private in Thought and Practice: Perspectives on a Grand Dichotomy* (Chicago: University of Chicago Press, 1997).

16. These issues are discussed in Jeremy Webber and Colin Macleod, eds., *Between Consenting Peoples: Political Community and the Meaning of Consent* (Vancouver: University of British Columbia Press, 2010).

17. While we might agree on many things, society cannot be built on any single vision of the good life. Ideas and practices which produce conflict, coincidence, centralization, and diffusion intermingle throughout the land. This is healthy because it signals freedom, autonomy, self-restraint, and self-determination have a foothold in broad parts of our law. Yet there are problems in our midst. These patterns must be extended because too many people don't enjoy sufficient freedom. Thus, we need to add more considerations to political and legal affairs, to ensure that ever-widening groups of people can enjoy the benefits of a free and democratic society.

life. To reiterate, all law and politics are provisional, contingent, and contextual. Law and love are not co-extensive either; these ideas and practices overlap, intersect, and conflict. Love and law occupy concurrently discrete, separate, distinct, related, parallel, corresponding and cross-cutting spheres. The relation is complicated, but there is a relationship. Thus, rather than banish love from legal practice, I am merely arguing that love deserves a much greater place in Canada's constitutional law, even as I recognize its limits.[18]

With this backdrop, I will now discuss how the language of love, in relation to aboriginal and treaty rights in section 35(1) of our constitution, could provide new avenues of protection and insight in this regard.

Love, Aboriginal, and Treaty Rights: Section 35(1) and Indigenous Traditions

HOW CANADIAN LAW INCORPORATES INDIGENOUS LAWS RELATED TO LOVE INTO ITS FRAMEWORK

Aboriginal and treaty rights in Canada's constitution incorporate political and legal traditions from indigenous communities. The Supreme Court of Canada, citing Professor Mark Walters, observed that "the essence of aboriginal rights is their bridging of aboriginal and non-aboriginal cultures." In *R. v. Vanderpeet*, the Court wrote:

> The challenge of defining aboriginal rights stems from the fact that they are rights peculiar to the meeting of two vastly

18. My argument is that love can and should play a more prominent role in understanding rights and freedoms, even as I fully acknowledge that politics and law will never solely or principally be consumed by this concern. To banish love from politics would ignore who we are as human beings, and would see us lose a crucial legal resource.

dissimilar legal cultures; consequently there will always be a question about which legal culture is to provide the vantage point from which rights are to be defined. . . . a morally and politically defensible conception of aboriginal rights will incorporate both legal perspectives.[19]

This important precedent means that Canada's law dealing with indigenous peoples is intersocietal.[20] Canadian constitutional law combines legal perspectives from common law and indigenous legal sources, practices, customs, and traditions. Of course this happens when treaties are signed or interpreted. Both parties' legal perspectives are central to determining an agreement's meaning. The same holds true when recognizing unextinguished rights, which have never surrendered through a treaty. Indigenous law must be referenced in such cases since such rights rest on preexisting indigenous authorities. This insight opens up significant space for indigenous legal principles in Canada's highest law. This process is particularly relevant when indigenous laws reinforce love. Indigenous principles and practices concerning love could be incorporated by reference, as law, when considering standards in cases and issues involving indigenous peoples throughout Canada.

For example, when indigenous peoples signed treaties with the Crown in Canada, love was frequently invoked, even in the face of sharp disagreements. The earliest recorded treaty with the French, in 1645, illustrates this sentiment. After significant tension which included loss of life, in the midst of a dramatic treaty ceremony with elaborate gifts, an Iroquois Chief named Kiotseaeton seized

19. R. v. Vanderpeet, [1996] 2 S.C.R. 507 at para. 42.
20. See John Borrows and Len Rotman, "The Sui Generis Nature of Aboriginal Rights: Does it Make a Difference?," *University of Alberta Law Review* 36 (1997), 9; John Borrows, *Canada's Indigenous Constitution* (Toronto: University of Toronto Press, 2010).

a French and Anishinaabe leader by the arms.[21] As he linked them
together, he said:

> Here is the knot that binds us inseparably. Nothing can part
> us . . . Even if lightening were to fall upon us, it could not sepa-
> rate us; for if it cuts off the arm that hold you to us, we will at
> once seize each other by the other arm.[22]

At this and similar gatherings, French, Anishinaabe, and other indigenous treaty partners frequently exchanged children to be raised in
one another's villages as a sign of their love and trust toward one
another. This led to a successful intersocietal compact which further
created economies, cultures, and family relationships that blended
aspects of each group's values. At a later date a French leader summed
up the results of this love: "We sustain ourselves only through the
goodwill of the [Indians] . . . it is the affection that they have for us
that has preserved [French] Canada until now."[23]

21. For greater context for linking arms together as a treaty expression of love and affection,
    see Robert A. Williams Jr., *Linking Arms Together: American Indian Treaty of Visions of Law
    and Peace 1600–1800* (New York: Oxford University Press, 1997). Further background on
    treaty-making in this period is found in Richard White, *The Middle Ground: Indians, Empires
    and Republics in the Great Lakes Region 1650–1815*; William Fenton, "Structure, Continuity
    and Change in the Process of Iroquois Treaty Making," in *The History and Culture of Iroquois
    Diplomacy*, ed. Francis Jennings et al. (Syracuse, NY: Syracuse University Press, 1985), 3;
    Victor Lytwyn, "A Dish with One Spoon: The Shared Hunting Grounds Agreement in the
    Great Lakes and St. Lawrence Valley," in *Papers of the Twenty-Eighth Algonquian Conference*,
    ed. David Pentland (Winnipeg: University of Manitoba, 1997), 210.

22. The person who recorded the treaty then observed, "And thereupon he turned around,
    and caught the French man and the Algonquin by their two other arms—holding them so
    closely that he seemed unwilling to ever leave them." Jennings et al., *The History and Culture
    of Iroquois Diplomacy*,141.

23. Louis-Antoine Bougainville, *Ecrits sur la Canada Memoires, Journal-Lettres* (Pelican/
    Klincksiek, 1993), 83, 96, 30, 166, 253, in *The Great Peace of Montreal of 1701: French-
    native Diplomacy in the Seventeenth Century*, ed. David Pentland (Montreal: McGill-Queen's
    University Press, 2001), 181–182.

The first indigenous treaties with the British also deployed similar metaphors and actions to express these feelings.[24] For example, in the 1700s, treaties of trade caused the Hudson's Bay Company governor to pledge "that he loves the Indians and will be kind to them."[25] Love was most welcome because of the vulnerability each group felt in their new relationship. Elaborate ceremonies of peace and the mutual exchange of food, clothing, kin, and accommodation between the parties made love manifest.[26] The main symbol of love and mutual aid for the British/indigenous alliance was a large wampum belt with figures representing twenty-four nations,[27] including

24. John Borrows, "Wampum at Niagara: The Royal Proclamation, Canadian Legal History, and Self-Government," in *Aboriginal and Treaty Rights in Canada*, ed. Michael Asch (Vancouver: University of British Columbia Press, 1997), 155.

25. Glyndwr Williams, ed., *Andrew Graham's Observations on Hudson's Bay 1767–1791* (London: Hudson's Bay Record Society, 1969), 316, quoted in Arthur Ray, J. R. Miller, and Frank Tough, *Bounty and Benevolence: A History of Saskatchewan Treaties* (Montreal: McGill-Queen's Press, 2000), 6.

26. For a discussion of these ceremonies, see Wilbur R. Jacobs, *Diplomacy and Indian Gifts: Anglo-French Rivalry Along the Ohio and North-west Frontiers* (Stanford, CA: Stanford University Press, 1950).

27. Sir William Johnson, himself, in introducing this belt at Niagara in 1764, captured the mutual aid and care embedded in this agreement when he stated:

Brothers of the Western Nations, Sachems, Chiefs and Warriors; You have now been here for several days, during which time we have frequently met to renew and Strengthen our Engagements and you have made so many Promises of your Friendship and Attachment to the English that there now remains for us only to exchange the great Belt of the Covenant Chain that we may not forget our mutual Engagements.

I now therefore present you the great Belt by which I bind all your Western Nations together with the English, and I desire that you will take fast hold of the same, and never let it slip, to which end I desire that after you have shewn this belt to all Nations you will fix one end of it to the Chipeweighs at St. Mary's whilst the other end remains at my house, and moreover I desire that you will never listen to any news which comes to any other Quarter. If you do it, it may shake the Belt.

C. Flick, ed., *The Papers of Sir William Johnson*, vol. 2 (Albany: University of the State of New York Press, 1925), 309–310.

the British, linking arms together.[28] The metaphor pledged that if any party needed assistance they would merely have to pull on the arm of the one next to them, and they would come to their aid in peace, friendship, and respect. This treaty turned 250 years old in 2014 and is one of our country's most significant constitutional moments. Two thousand Indians from twenty-two nations gathered at Niagara with the British in 1764, after the Seven Years War.[29] At this two-month gathering the parties pledged that their future relationships would be built on love rather than conquest, force, and contempt.[30] Images from both the Twenty-four Nations wampum belt of 1764 and the 1764 belt prominently display each wampum holder's heart.[31]

28. "The two memoranda (wampum) which they hold; the one being a pledge of perpetual friendship between the N.A. Indians, and the British Nations, and was delivered to the Tribe as a Council convened for that purpose, by Sir William Johnson, at Niagara in 1764." Thomas G. Anderson, superintendent of Indian affairs at Manitoulin Island, Indian Department Report, *Report of Indian Affairs* (1845) at 269, described it as follows:

> On the other wampum belt is marked at one end a hieroglyphic denoting Quebec on this continent, on the other, is a ship with its bow towards Quebec; betwixt those two objects are wove 24 Indians, one holding the cable of the vessel with his right, and so on, until the figure on the extreme left rests his foot on the land at Quebec. Their traditional account of this is, that at the time it was delivered to them (1764) Sir William Johnson promised, in the name of the Government, that those Tribes should continue to receive presents as long as the sun would shine . . . and if ever the ship came across the Great salt lake without a full cargo, these tribes should pull lustily at the cable until they brought her over full of presents.

29. For further historical context, see Colin Calloway, *The Scratch of a Pen: 1763 and the Transformation of North American* (New York: Penguin, 2006).

30. Jeffery Hewitt, "Honour and Community: Indigenous Peoples and the Constitution," *Supreme Court Law Review* 67 (2014), 259.

31. Alan Corbiere, "'Their Own Forms of Which They Take the Most Notice': Diplomatic Metaphors and Symbolism on Wampum Belts," in *Anishinaabewin Niiwin: Four Rising Winds 2013: A Selection from the Proceedings of the 2013 Anishinaabewin Niiwin Multidisciplinary Culture Conference, held in Sudbury, Ontario*, ed. Alan Corbiere (M'Chigeeng, ON: Ojibwe Cultural Foundation, 2014), 47–64.

Love was also prominently a part of Canada's subsequent pre-confederation treaties with the Anishinaabe and other indigenous nations. My own great-great-grandfather signed a treaty which promised other indigenous peoples perpetual rights on our lands because of "the natural love and affection we have for our Indian brothers."[32] Indigenous peoples also spoke of their love for the Crown and her subjects, while the Crown spoke about its love of the Indians in various public settings. In one prominent example, a Mohawk chief welcomed an English leader through treaty by proclaiming: "My son, you are now flesh of our flesh and bone of our bone. . . . After what has passed this day you are now one of us through an old strong law and custom. My son you have nothing to fear. We are now under the same obligations to love, support and defend you that we are to love and defend one another. Therefore you are to consider us as one of our people."[33]

Post-confederation treaties also contain numerous references to love. The oral histories of the numbered treaties which stretch from Ontario to the Northwest Territories are peppered with pledges which speak about the heart.[34] For instance, during Treaty 4 negotiations, when Anishinaabe leader "The Gambler" discussed sharing his peoples' lands with future settlers he spoke of love. While he was very upset that the Crown had not restrained the Hudson's Bay in his territory, he nevertheless dealt with this sharp disagreement

---

32. Treaty 80 registered on August, 4, 1854, in *Canada: Indian Treaties and Surrenders, from 1680–1890*, vol. 1 (Ottawa: Printer to the Queen's Most Excellent Majesty, 1891–1912; repr. Toronto: Coles, 1971), 209.

33. James Miller, *Compact, Contract, Covenant: Aboriginal Treaty-Making in Canada* (Toronto: University of Toronto Press, 2009), 10.

34. Alexander Morris, *The Treaties of Canada with the Indians of Manitoba and the North-West Territories, Including the Negotiations on Which They were Based, and Other Information Relating Thereto* (Saskatoon: Fifth House Publishers, 1991), 40, 59, 60, 72, 92–95, 100, 109–110, 113, 115, 117, 174, 191, 199, 200–201, 203–204, 209, 234–238.

within a framework of love. He said, referring to both the aboriginal and other people gathered at this ceremony,

> Look at these children that are sitting around here and also at the tents, who are just like the image of my kindness. There are different kinds of grass growing here that is just like those sitting around here. There is no difference. Even from the American land they are here, but we love them all the same, and when the white skin comes here from far away I love him all the same. I am telling you what our love and kindness is.[35]

At Treaty Six, Sweetgrass took the treaty commissioner's hand and physically placed it on his heart. He then said, "When I hold your hand and touch my heart, let us be as one; use your utmost to help me and help my children that they may prosper."[36]

Very significant legal implications flow from references to love found in Canada's treaty experience. The love expressed in these agreements is a part of Canadian law because courts must take account of the aboriginal perspective on the meaning of the right at stake when interpreting Canada's constitution.[37] Of course, love is not the only principle underlying the treaties and other relationships indigenous peoples experience in Canada. There is also significant evidence of hate, racism, duplicity, greed, anger, and expediency in their interactions with others.[38] Thus, we have choice

---

35. "The Gambler," Qu'Appelle Treaty, Fort Qu'Appelle, Saskatchewan, September 12, 1874, in Morris, *The Treaties of Canada with the Indians of Manitoba and the North-West Territories*, 100.

36. Morris, *The Treaties of Canada with the Indians of Manitoba and the North-West Territories*, 191.

37. R. v. Sparrow, [1990] 1 S.C.R. 1075 at 1112.

38. Royal Commission on Aboriginal Peoples, *Report of the Royal Commission on Aboriginal Peoples, Vol. 2, Restructuring the Relationship* (Ottawa: Supply and Services, 1996), 1–62.

about which principles we should emphasize when applying these agreements and pursuing contemporary policies today. We can choose to interpret treaties and other legal rights in the light of love, or we can choose some other, less lofty goal.[39] Remember, this is a constitution we are interpreting.

Fortunately, the Supreme Court of Canada insists that in considering aboriginal and treaty rights we must apply an interpretation which upholds the honor of the Crown.[40] The Court has said that "honour of the Crown . . . infuses the processes of treaty making and treaty interpretation. In making and applying treaties, [it says] the Crown must act with honor and integrity, avoiding even the appearance of "sharp dealing."[41] The Court has written that "this principle goes beyond treaty rights in section 35(1) of the Constitution, and also applies to Aboriginal rights—those rights not affected by treaties."[42] It declared that "the controlling question in all situations involving section 35(1) is what is required

---

39. For a book that interprets treaties in light of the principle of honor, see Michael Asch, *On Being Here to Stay* (Vancouver: University of British Columbia Press, 2014).

40. In R. v. Marshall, [1999] 3 S.C.R. 456 at para 14, the Court wrote:

> The Indian parties did not, for all practical purposes, have the opportunity to create their own written record of the negotiations. Certain assumptions are therefore made about the Crown's approach to treaty making (honourable) which the Court acts upon in its approach to treaty interpretation (flexible) as to the existence of a treaty . . . the completeness of any written record . . . and the interpretation of treaty terms once found to exist. The bottom line is the Court's obligation is to "choose from among the various possible interpretations of the *common* intention [at the time the treaty was made] the one which best reconciles" the [First Nation] interests and those of the Crown.

41. Mikisew Cree First Nation v. Canada (Minister of Canadian Heritage), [2005] 3 S.C.R. 388 at para. 33; Grassy Narrows First Nation v. Ontario (Natural Resources), [2014] S.C.C. 48 at para. 50–51.

42. Ibid., at para. 51: "The honour of the Crown exists as a source of obligation independently of treaties as well, of course." See also Tsilhqot'in Nation v. British Columbia, [2014] S.C.C. 44 at para. 78.

to maintain the honour of the Crown and to effect reconciliation between the Crown and the Aboriginal peoples with respect to the interests at stake."[43]

Given the strong references to love in Canada's indigenous history, it is not unreasonable to consider love as a legal principle when dealing with aboriginal and treaty rights in Canada. The Supreme Court of Canada has repeatedly affirmed that historic treaties and other rights are to be interpreted in a liberal manner, in a manner that they would naturally be understood by the Indians, resolving any ambiguities in their favor.[44] Love, as a treaty principle, fits these frameworks.[45]

---

43. Ibid., at para. 62, citing Haida Nation v. British Columbia (Minister of Forests), [2004] 3 S.C.R. 511 at para. 43–45.

44. R. v. White and Bob (1964), 50 D.L.R. (2d) 613 (B.C.C.A.); affd. (1965) 52 D.L.R. (2d) 481n; R. v. Taylor and Williams (1981), 34 O.R. (2d) 360 (Ont. C.A.); R. v. Simon (1985) 24 D.L.R. (4th) 390; R. v. Sioui, [1990] 1 S.C.R. 1025; R. v. Horseman, [1990] 1 S.C.R. 901 at 907; R. v. Badger, [1996] 1 S.C.R. 771 at paras. 4 and 41; R. v. Sundown, [1999] 1 S.C.R. 393 (S.C.C.) at para. 24–25; R. v. Marshall, [1999] 3 S.C.R. 456 at paras. 9–14; R. v. Marshall, [1999] 3 S.C.R. 533 at para. 19; R. v. Marshall, R. v. Bernard, [2005] 2 S.C.R. 220 at para. 26; R. v. Morris, [2006] 2 S.C.R. 915 at para. 19.

45. The Supreme Court already deploys broad categories in this field which, in other areas of law, might be in many circumstances considered moral as opposed to legal principles. The Court uses concepts like honor, faith, reconciliation, fairness, reasonableness, and generous interpretative frameworks. These principles are regularly deployed as precise reasons for decision in major cases. Love is not completely out of place in such a list. It is not so far removed from reconciliation, good faith, and honor.

In some broad sense Canadians have generally demonstrated capacities for empathy by placing rights and freedoms of others ahead of our own, at least on constitutional paper. This includes the rights of aboriginal peoples. This capacity for self-restraint is one reason why sovereignty is generally constrained by constitutional rights. When rights are applied, the majority forgoes its claim to some public good to guarantee access to such resources by groups or individuals with less political power. While this aspect of rights is also explained by self-interest (a majority today could be a minority tomorrow), somewhere in this mix rights can also be explained by reference to the love that human beings have toward one another.

Anishinaabe Love and the Law: Zaagi'idiwin—A Legal Principle Explained

HOW ANISHINAABE LAW CHARACTERIZES LOVE

To more fully apply indigenous principles in a Canadian legal framework we must develop stronger understandings of how indigenous peoples characterize love in regulating behavior and resolving disputes. This means I must now give a necessarily brief description of indigenous law as it relates to love to further illustrate the implications of the court's constitutional jurisprudence. I will do so by reference to the legal tradition which I have been discussing throughout this essay: the Anishinaabe tradition.[46] Anishinaabe people are the fourth largest tribal group in the United States, after the Navajo, Cherokee, and Lakota nations.[47] There are approximately 100,000 Anishinaabe people in Canada and the United States. We live within the Great Lakes watershed, surrounding large parts of Lakes Superior, Huron, and Michigan. We also occupy the farmlands and woodlands north of Lake Ontario and Lake Erie, and live on reservations in the forests and prairies of northern Minnesota, Manitoba, and North Dakota.[48]

Anishinaabe law has many sources, particularly when viewed in its wider North American context. It is derived from constitutions, statutes, bylaws, tribal court decisions, community deliberations, persuasion, counseling together, songs, stories, ceremonies,

---

46. The Anishinaabe are also called Ojibwe or Chippewa people. I am from the Chippewas of the Nawash First Nation Reserve, which is also called Neyaashiinigmiing, or the Cape Croker Indian Reserve. This is a reserve of over two thousand people on the shores of Lake Huron, four hours north of Toronto, on the Bruce Peninsula.

47. US Census Bureau, The American Indian and Alaska Native Population: 2010 17 tbl. 7 (2010), http://www.census.gov/prod/cen2010/briefs/c2010br-10.pdf.

48. See Helen Hornbeck Tanner, *Atlas of Great Lakes Indian History* (Norman: University of Oklahoma Press, 1982), 58–59.

teachings ascribed to the Creator, and the land itself. Like all law in North America, Anishinaabe law is complex yet practical. While the place of love in Anishinaabe law could be examined from any one of these legal bases, I will focus on a source less familiar to most Canadian legal practitioners: the land itself. I do so to identify a pattern present within many indigenous legal orders, reasoning which occurs by reference to the natural environment. This mode of legal reasoning deserves much greater emphasis because we risk misconstruing indigenous law if we do not attend to this source. I worry about assimilation if indigenous laws are only framed in terms which correspond to Canadian legal practices. Thus the need to sometimes highlight differences. However, it is important to stress that this following analysis rests on only one layer of Anishinaabe law. A fuller application of Anishinaabe law would also have to engage other sources.

I also make this point to signal that the practice of Anishinaabe law, like all legal traditions, is subject to differing interpretations, and also to contradictory, cross-cutting and convergent influences. Indigenous peoples have choices available to them when they practice law. Consensus can be fleeting. This is a strength found in all legal orders, as long as momentary acquiescence occurs at critical points in a community's legal life.[49] For instance, Canadian law largely consists of inconsistent, incongruous, and differing points of view. Judges issues majority and dissenting opinions. Parliament has an official opposition, and we have recently experienced the fractiousness of minority governments. Yet when Parliament passes a statute, or a court issues a decision, there is at least initial

---

49. Jeremy Webber, "The Meanings of Consent," in *Between Consenting Peoples: Political Community and the Meaning of Consent,* ed. Jeremy Webber and Colin Macleod (Vancouver: University of British Columbia Press, 2010), 3–41; Jeremy Webber, "The Grammar of Customary Law," *McGill Law Journal* 54 (2009), 579–626.

agreement before the parties all run off in a thousand directions, giving their own spin to what was decided. Legal disagreements are healthy because they allow people with different points of view to live together and bring their own opinions to life's regulatory and dispute resolution contexts. Indigenous law also embodies these complexities, requiring a clear declaration that my interpretation of what follows is not necessarily determinative. Though I believe the following account of Anishinaabe law is accurate, reasonable, and evenhanded, as far as I understand this law,[50] I freely acknowledge that appeal to other sources within Anishinaabe jurisprudence will produce further insights.[51]

Love is one of the Anishinaabe peoples' seven grandfather teachings, which are *nibwaakaawin* (wisdom), *minaadendiwin* (respect), *aakwaadiziwin* (bravery), *dbaadendiziwin* (humility), *gweyakwaadiziwin* (honesty), *debwewin* (truth), and *zaagi'idiwin* (love).[52] I will discuss this last principle zaagi'idiwin, as drawn from the land to address Anishinaabe legal reasoning processes described above, and to apply this concept to protecting Anishinaabe reserves from alienation and diminishment.

As noted, Anishinaabe people practice law by reference to the natural world. The Anishinaabe have long taken direction about

---

50. Debewin, in Anishinaabemowin, means to tell the truth, as far as I understand it.
51. See the work of Matthew Fletcher, for example, in developing Anishinaabe positivist law in law-review articles and Anishinaabe tribal court decisions. For example, see Re. Kern, Judicial Commission of the Grand Traverse Band of Ottawa and Chippewa Indians at https://turtletalk.files.wordpress.com/2013/05/kern-final-opinion.pdf (applying principles of mino-bimaadiziwn for removal of a tribal court judge); Spurr v. v Nottawaseppi Huron Band of Potawatomi Indians, Huron Potawatomi tribal court (applying mnobmadzewen to an electoral issue) at http://turtletalk.files.wordpress.com/2013/05/spurr-v-nottawaseppi-huron-band-of-potawatomi-indians.pdf.
52. The Anishinaabe call these practices the "seven grandfathers." For more information about these ideas, see Eddie Benton Benai, *The Mishomis Book* (Hayward, WI: Indian Country Communications, 1988), 64.

how to live through interactions with and observations of the environment. They regulate their behavior and resolve their disputes by drawing guidance from what they see in the behavior of the sun, moon, stars, winds, waves, trees, birds, animals, and other natural phenomenon. The Anishinaabe word for this concept is gikinawaabiwin.[53] We can also use the word "akinoomaage," which is formed from two roots: "aki" and "noomaage." "Aki" means earth and "noomaage" means to point toward and take direction from. As Anishinaabe draw analogies from our surroundings and appropriately apply or distinguish what we see, we learn about how love, and how we should live in our lands. Reason can be developed by analogy in Anishinaabe law, just as in the common law: parallel situations are correlated, dissimilar situations are distinguished. The difference is that this Anishinaabe legal process occurs by reading the land, in addition to reading past cases, as may occur in tribal or other courts.[54]

One of the sources of environmental legal insight comes from watching the rivers flow, the grasses grow, and the sun shine. In fact, one of the strongest symbols use in describing the importance of indigenous treaties is "as long as the shine shines, the grass grows, and the river flows."[55] This representation, while possessing deeper

53. Anishinaabe language professor and linguistic Brenda Fairbanks traced the etymology of "gikinoo'amaage," as follows (personal correspondence, January 17, 2014):

- gikinaw—learn, know, recognize
- I—by instrument
- 'amaw—applicative
- ge—detransitive (to general people)

54. For a more general discussion of analogical reasoning, see Cass R. Sunstein, "On Analogical Reasoning," *Harvard Law Review* 106 (1993), 741.

55. For a discussion of this concept in law, see Charles Wilkinson and John Volkman, "Judicial Review of Indian Treaty Abrogation: As Long as Water Flows, or Grass Grows upon the Earth—How Long a Time is That?," *California Law Review* 63 (1975), 601. An early use of a similar phrase is found in a treaty made by William Penn with the Conestoga in 1701.

meaning,[56] emphasizes the perpetual nature of agreements to live together in peace, friendship, and respect.[57] Thus, we can more fully understand Anishinaabe treaties by examining how Anishinaabe people describe these natural processes.

The Anishinaabe word for the mouth of a river is "saugeen." There is a Saugeen First Nation in Manitoba and a Saginaw, Michigan, and my own people are also called the Saugeen Ojibwe on the Saugeen or Bruce Peninsula in Ontario. Canada's sixth

See Kevin Kenny, *Peaceable Kingdom Lost: The Paxton Boys and the Destruction of William Penn's Holy Experiment* (New York: Oxford University Press, 2009), 15: "As long as the Sun and Moon shall endure." Benjamin Franklin reported this treaty as saying, "As long as the sun shall shine, or the waters run in the rivers," in Jared Sparks, ed., *The Works of Benjamin Franklin: Autobiography, pt. 2* (T. MacCoun, 1882). Other associations between treaties and the phrase are found in Harold Cardinal and Walter Hildebrandt, *Treaty Elders of Saskatchewan: Our Dream Is That Our Peoples Will One Day Be Clearly Recognized as Nations* (Calgary: University of Calgary Press, 2000), 20; Treaty 7 Elders and Tribal Council with Walter Hildebrandt, Sarah Carter, and Dorothy First Rider, *The True Spirit and Original Intent of Treaty 7* (Montreal-Kingston: McGill-Queen's Press, 1996), 133; Rene Fumoleau, *As Long as This Land Shall Last: A History of Treaty 8 and 11* (Toronto: McClelland and Stewart, 1976), 74, 133, 240, 257, 314, 340, 502; Arthur Ray, J. R. Miller, and Frank Tough, *Bounty and Benevolence: A History of Saskatchewan Treaties* (Montreal: McGill-Queen's Press, 2000), 116–117. For a contrary view about questioning this relationship of this phrase to treaties, see Sharon Venne, "Understanding Treaty Six: An Indigenous Perspective," in *Aboriginal and Treaty Rights in Canada: Essays on Law, Equality, and Respect for Difference*, ed. Michael Asch (Vancouver: University of British Columbia Press, 1997), 173 at 194.

56. For example, see pages 5–14 of Deanna Christensen, *Ahtahkakoop: The Epic Account of a Plains Cree Head Chief, His People, and Their Struggle for Survival, 1816–1896* (Shell Lake, Sask.: Ahtahkakoop Publishing, 2000) for a brief discussion of laws related to the sun, waters, and earth. For an ingenious literary treatment of this idea, see Thomas King, *Green Grass, Running Water* (Toronto: Harper Collins, 1993).

57. For example, when Alexander Morris proposed Treaty 6, he said, "What I trust and hope we will do is not for today or tomorrow only; what I promise and what I believe and hope you will take, is to last as long as that sun shines and yonder river flows." Alexander Morris, *The Treaties of Canada with the Indians of Manitoba and the North-West Territories, Including the Negotiations on Which They Were Based, and Other Information Relating Thereto* (Saskatoon: Fifth House Publishers, 1991), 202; see similar words in relation to Treaty 3 at page 51. This phrase was also used in an 1818 treaty with the Ojibway. See J. R. Miller, *Compact, Contract, Covenant: Aboriginal Treaty-Making in Canada* (Toronto: University of Toronto Press, 2009), 101.

largest city is called Mississauga, or Michi-zaagiin, which describes a large river mouth in our language. The mouth of a river is a place of great life. In our territory, powerful waters carry nutrients off the hundreds of thousands of acres of land into Lake Huron. These waters carry organic and other life-giving matter, and help nourish a more abundant life. Fish, birds, plants, and animals gather at great river mouths in substantial numbers to draw on the sustaining energy they provide.

The Ojibwe have a word that sounds similar to zaagiin, which is "zaagi'idiwin"—the word for love. While the words have different roots, and are etymologically unrelated,[58] many modern speakers draw strong parallels between them, including elders on my reserve. They explain that rivers can be studied to identify analogies which provide standards about how we should extend our love to others. Thus, Dr. Basil Johnston taught me that love, like a stream, should carry sustenance. It should continually flow to support those around us. Its currents should be strong and lay down layers of nourishment, as the forces of life course through us and strengthen others. Love is about the free flow of support to others. It allows us to sustain those who gather around us. It creates a more rich,

---

58. Anishinaabe language professor and linguistic Brenda Fairbanks explained the technical meaning of these words as follows (personal correspondence, January 17, 2014):
- Zaagiing and zaagi'idiwin are based upon two different roots and are not related.
  - zaag—out, stick out
  - zaagi'—stingy
- zaagikweni—"sticks his head out," for example for root zaag-.
- Zaagi' has replaced the old word "dabaan" for "love" for many Ojibwe dialects, but remains in some and in other related languages like Kickapoo and meskwaki. But zaagi' and zaagitoon are words for "be stingy with him" and "be stingy with it" and are unrelated to zaagiing.
- Though these two roots look alike, they are not the same and not usually considered to be related. In Ojibwe, similarity in look does not indicate degree of relatedness.

varied, diverse and abundant life. For elders like Basil Johnston, this is implied in their use of the word "zaagiin," which means "to extend or stick out." Love should be perceptible; it should swell, expand, and project itself into our relationships. Perhaps in keeping with their different etymologies, which cause some speakers to blur distinctions because of aural similarities, zaagi' also connotes a kind of exclusivity, even stinginess, which signifies that love must not be dissipated. Love in this context requires focused delivery, with a directed transfer through defined channels, analogous to a river's mouth.

As noted above, when law is practiced in any tradition we recognize interpretation rarely rests on one case, statute, or interpretive phrase or word. This is particularly so when linguistic and folk etymologies do not coincide. Therefore we must triangulate sources, and compare and contrast interpretations, to ensure we understand the details and broader picture of what a system's legal standards require. Words and concepts are used in different ways, for varied purposes, depending on their context. The same is true with Anishinaabe law. Thus, we must consider other ways of expressing love in Anishinaabemowin.

As a result, we could look to other words deploying zaagiin and zaagi'idiwin. For instance, Anishinaabe law looks to how the grasses grow to develop standards for judgment and criteria for decision making. Anishinaabe lawyer Kekek (Jason Stark) notes that "Zaagi'bagaa" references energy flows found in budding, emergent leaves.[59] He says, "As a flower begins to bud, the love and beauty inside emerges or casts its self out."[60] For him, another derivation

59. My special thanks are giving to Jason Stark, Kekek, for reminding me of some of these teachings, and bringing others to my attention for the first time. Miigwech.
60. Ibid.

of zaagi' is Zaagajiiwegaabawikwe, which is his daughter's name. It refers to the casting of love through the rays of the sun. Again, we see that flows of energy, sustenance, and power are part of the idea of love, as drawn from these words.

"Zhawenim" is another Anishinaabe word used to describe love. It means to have compassion or affection for another in one's thoughts and mind. It has a connotation of bestowing kindness, mercy, and aid. It includes ideas of pity, empathy, and deep unconditional love. Sometimes the Creator is called Gizhemnido, the Compassionate Spirit, in addition to Gichi-manidoo, the Great Spirit. "Zhawenim" does not have the connotations of stinginess that are attached to "zaagi'idiwin." "Zhawenim" also has a place in other key Anishinaabe relationships. For instance, my friend Kekek notes that "zhawenjige" is another derivation of "zhawenim."[61] It means to hunt. We hear the word used in hunting and harvesting songs. When we sing "zhawenim izhichige," it means "you will be pitied, or have mercy placed upon you in your actions and what you are doing." The idea behind this word is that when we acknowledge our relations with the world, and our responsibilities to each other, then we will all be blessed or find love and compassion. We will be nourished, sustained, and taken care of. The idea of zhawenjige is said to be part of an old treaty the Anishinaabe made with the animals.[62] As long as we love them they will provide for us, and teach us about love and how to live well in the world. Our clans or dodeems, of which mine is the otter, are said to be particularly important in experiencing and understanding this love.

---

61. Ibid.
62. John Borrows, *Recovering Canada: The Resurgence of Indigenous Law* (Toronto: University of Toronto Press, 2002), 46.

Anishinaabe Love and Law: Zaagiin/Zaagi'idiwin—
A Legal Principle Applied

HOW INDIGENOUS LAND AND RESOURCE RIGHTS MIGHT FARE IF CANADA'S CONSTITUTION REFERENCED ANISHINAABE LAWS

Now that we have identified the possible place of love in an aboriginal or treaty rights framework, we can now apply this principle to a particular indigenous issue: indigenous peoples' relationship with the land. Thus, I will now take the first steps in sketching out the application of Anishinaabe legal principles to the recognition and affirmation of Anishinaabe land and resource rights. I do this in remembrance that such principles could be incorporated as aboriginal and treaty rights within Canada's constitution.

Applying Zaagiin/Zaagi'idiwin: The Context

In discussing indigenous peoples' challenges related to land, we must contextualize them within a broader contemporary framework. Remedies must be applied which match the breadth of the problem indigenous peoples face. This will help us properly apply zaagi'idiwn to indigenous land and resources rights. This context first reveals that indigenous peoples' lives are drastically shorter than other Canadians. They are marked by more suffering as measured by considerably higher rates of poverty, injury, and incarceration, and significantly lower levels of education, income, and health.[63]

---

63. The federal government spends approximately $9,000 per capita on First Nations people, which is generally the sole basis of government support. An average Canadian receives $7,300 from the federal government and $9,200 from the provincial government, which is $16,500 in total aid. Thus, Indians receive approximately 45 percent in government support compared to the average Canadian. This number is even more troubling when we recognize that services to First Nations are more expensive because of their remote locations, and that First Nations cannot access many provincial funding sources. Numbers are drawn from

Anishinaabe laws related to love must address the effects of Canadian legal action. This includes the 1876 Indian Act, which has assimilation as its explicit goal.[64] Its main provisions have not changed in over 138 years. It was designed to separate indigenous peoples from whom and what we love. It is explicitly aimed at preventing us from freely governing ourselves.[65] It seeks to change how we relate to land.[66] Recent proposals seek to deepen these changes by making Indian land alienable to non-Indians.[67] In addition, the Indian Act denies us powers to expand First Nations citizenship.[68] This echoes the forced exile First Nations encountered when they married non-Indian men.[69] This cut off great strength from our communities for close to one hundred years, and the problem is still not adequately addressed. The Indian Act also restrains commerce[70] and education.[71] This is deeply troubling, given what transpired in residential schools. Residential schools were institutions of forced assimilation, where people were too frequently abused. These schools attempted to eradicate indigenous language, culture, and tradition, as the federal government teamed up with churches to undermine indigenous peoples' own

Mark Milke, "Taxpayers Are Generous to First Nations," December 13, 2013, http://www.fraserinstitute.org/research-news/news/display.aspx?id=20707.

64. John Tobias, "Protection, Civilization and Assimilation: An Outline History of Canada's Indian Policy," in *Sweet Promises: A Reader on Indian-White Relations in Canada*, ed. James Miller (Toronto: University of Toronto Press, 1991), 127.

65. Indian Act, R.S.C. 1985, c. I-5, ss. 18–41. [PE: I'm unsure what the highlighting is calling out. Use of "ss." for section rather than symbol? Or discrepancy with singular/plural?]

66. Indian Act, R.S.C. 1985, c. I-5, ss. 74–80.

67. Tom Flanagan, Christopher Alcantra, and Andre Le Dressay, *Beyond the Indian Act: Restoring Aboriginal Property Rights* (Montreal: McGill-Queen's Press, 2010).

68. Indian Act, R.S.C. 1985, c. I-5, ss. 5–17.

69. Pamela D. Palmater, *Beyond Blood: Rethinking Indigenous Identity* (Saskatoon: Purich Publishing Limited, 2011).

70. Indian Act, R.S.C. 1985, c. I-5 at ss. 87, 91–92.

71. Ibid., at ss. 114–122.

aspirations.[72] The Indian Act also applies most provincial laws to reserves, which leaves virtually no political space for First Nations laws.[73] In addition, provincial laws have given non-native people ownership of and access to our resources while limiting our own control and uses.[74] This is evident in fields such as hunting, fishing, mining, forestry, land-use planning, and numerous other resource regimes. These laws have impoverished most First Nations. We were denied the right to vote and enjoy the political franchise until 1960.[75] Until 1951 we were denied the right to hire lawyers and raise money to dispute our treatment. Some of our reserves were liquidated, and our people forcibly relocated. People were arbitrarily cut off from band lists and denied access to their families and homes.[76] To add fuel to this fire, children were removed

72. For a discussion of residential school's harsh effects on indigenous peoples, see John S. Milloy, *A National Crime: The Canadian Government and the Residential School System, 1879–1986* (Winnipeg: University of Manitoba Press, 1999); J. R. Miller, *Shingwauk's Vision: A History of Native Residential Schools* (Toronto: University of Toronto Press, 1996), 169–170.

73. For commentaries on the negative implications of provincial regulation on indigenous jurisdiction, see Leroy Littlebear, "Section 88 of the Indian Act and the Application of Provincial Laws to Indians," in *Governments in Conflict: Provinces and Indian Nations in Canada*, ed. J. Anthony Long and Menno Boldt (Toronto: University of Toronto Press, 1988), 175; Kerry Wilkins, "Still Crazy After All These Years': Section 88 of the Indian Act at Fifty," *Alberta Law Review* 38 (2000), 458; Kent McNeil, "Aboriginal Title and Section 88 of the Indian Act," *UBC Law Review* 34 (2000), 159.

74. Douglas Harris, *Landing Native Fisheries: Indian Reserves and Fishing Rights in British Columbia, 1849–1925* (Vancouver: University of British Columbia Press, 2008); Douglas Harris, *Fish, Law, and Colonialism: The Legal Capture of Salmon in British Columbia* (Vancouver: University of Toronto Press, 2001); Peggy Blair, *Lament for a First Nation: The Williams Treaties of Southern Ontario* (Vancouver: University of British Columbia Press, 2008); Frank Tough, *As Their Natural Resources Fail: Native People and the Economic History of Northern Manitoba, 1870–1930* (Vancouver: University of British Columbia Press, 1997); William Wicken, *The Colonization of Mi'kmaw Memory and History, 1794–1928: The King V. Gabriel Sylliboy* (Toronto: University of Toronto Press, 2012).

75. Robert Millen, ed., *Aboriginal Peoples and Electoral Reform in Canada, Volume 9* (Toronto: Dundurn Press, 1991).

76. While some of this was supposedly done with the best of intentions, others participated or turned a blind eye to these tragedies because of racist world views. While not clearly ethnic cleansing, for most native communities this history has led to analogous results. I must

from indigenous homes in the 1960s, in great numbers.[77] Even today, 50–80 percent of the children in government care in western Canada are indigenous children.[78] Indigenous peoples are living through a period of profound, extended, multigenerational trauma. Canadian law is a significant root cause of this national tragedy. So far, aboriginal and treaty rights related to love have not addressed these realities in any comprehensive manner.[79]

In the light of this experience, you might excuse some people for concluding that indigenous peoples are not loved. But this view is too simplistic. Most of these laws are born out of a modicum of care. Many Canadians truly believe that Indians would better off without reserves or distinct political recognition.[80] They want First Nations people to enjoy better lives. This view is dominant even today, judging by current legislative realities. While it helps that assimilation would reduce the obligations Canadians have to Indians, our current troubles may be partially traceable to Canadian's love of their fellow indigenous citizens. As noted earlier, love can be invoked in problematic ways; it can be oppressive, colonial, sexist, racist,

stress this is not the whole story. There is so much goodness, beauty, and decency in the world. However, to ignore the darkness that shaped and continues to shape Canada and our communities is to disregard reality too.

77. Chris Walmsley, *Protecting Aboriginal Children* (Vancouver: University of British Columbia Press, 2005); Sonia Harris-Short, *Aboriginal Child Welfare, Self-government and the Rights of Indigenous Children: Protecting the Vulnerable under International Law* (London: Ashgate, 2011).

78. Cindy Blackstock, Tara Prakash, John Loxley, and Fred Wien, *Wen:de: We are Coming to the Light of Day* (Vancouver: First Nations Family and Child Caring Society of Canada, 2005).

79. If Canada's constitution cannot address these issues, section 35(1) is essentially meaningless to indigenous peoples, and could even be considered a farce. Fortunately, as I have been suggesting, I do not believe we have to interpret our constitution in this way. While there are many cogent reasons to despair, given the courts' current jurisprudence and Parliament's obstructions and inaction, nothing in life is inevitable—including the continued oppression of indigenous peoples.

80. John Borrows, "Residential Schools, Respect and Responsibilities for Past Harms," *University of Toronto Law Journal* 64 (2014), 486.

and domineering. The problem with the way love is currently and historically channeled through legislative action is that it does not reaffirm the aspirations and desires of those to whom it is directed. Most First Nations people love their reserves and do not want to assimilate. While they want to more fully participate with their fellow citizens, they want this to occur in ways which reaffirm their own hopes and dreams. Acting out of concern for First Nations without recognizing self-determination is coercive. As we have discussed, love should never be coercive.

Zaagiin/Zaagi'idiwin and Land: Applying
Anishinaabe Law to the Facts

With this context in mind, we can now turn to Anishinaabe legal traditions to address the issue of aboriginal and treaty rights to land and resources. Anishinaabe law calls for the reversal of federal and provincial laws directed toward diminishing reserves and assimilating indigenous peoples. Anishinaabe legal principles reveal that Indian reserves and traditional territories should be places where love can flourish.

Anishinaabe and thus Canadian law must unleash energies which in human terms mimic the flowing of river at its mouth (zaagiin), the emerging force of leaves (zaagi'bagaa), and the streaming of rays from the sun (zaagajiiwegaaba). Remember these processes echo the language of treaties: "For as long as the rivers flow, the grass grows, and the sun shines." The English treaty language of cede, surrender, and release does not reflect these principles. The Indian Act does not contain this vision. These assimilative purposes direct energy away from the reserves rather than gathering its flow. Thus, the written treaties and the Indian Act cannot be consistent with Anishinaabe law, as contemplated by section 35(1) of Canada's constitution. The English translation of treaties and Parliament's statutory framework does not incorporate the living sense of the relationship. It ignores the sui generis, intersocietal bridge which indigenous legal traditions provide in framing Canada's highest laws. We should recognize and affirm principles like zaagiin, zaagi'bagaa, and zaagajiiwegaaba to enhance Anishinaabe land, resource, and treaty rights.

As Anishinaabe principles suggest, aboriginal rights law should encourage flows of social energy and material substance into our reserves from our surrounding territories. Section 35(1) should be directed to securing the nourishment, sustenance, and support indigenous peoples require. We must build up reserves, not tear them down. They must "stick out" (zaagiin). At the same time, reserves should only be seen as a small part of the Anishinaabe world. Consistent with Anishinaabe law, as recognized by our trea- ties, we have rights to access resources on and off these smaller enclaves. This is reflected in the Anishinaabe word for reserve: "ish- konigan." It means "leftovers." It was never intended that we should live on leftovers. Reserves should never be regarded as the sole site for make a living. Consistent with Anishinaabe legal principles anal- ogizing law to the life of a river's mouth, zaagiin, reserves should not be disconnected from surrounding territories, peoples, and econo- mies. They should be the site of connections. Richness, variety, and abundance should characterize their existence.[81]

A river's mouth does not only go in one direction. While water flows outward, fish, animals, and humans make their way up them to intermingle with other life. In early Canadian history rivers were a main source of travel, trade, recreation, and regenera- tion. Reserves often grew at these key junctures to facilitate these

---

81. Indigenous and other people share Canada's legal ecology. Reserves represent an important conduit in this ecosystem.

flows. While the modern geography of economic life has made backwaters of these communities, there is no doubt that significant resources continue to flow from most indigenous territories. Canada's prosperity is built on this fact; resources flow to Ottawa or provincial capitals, yet they are at a much greater distance than local reserves. Surely, we can direct some of this energy to local growth and well-being.

We need much better channels of access and distribution. We must build legal courses which allow indigenous peoples to navigate the economic and social currents which now bypass them. This requires changing our laws to place indigenous self-determination at the heart of their participation. Surges of energy, life, and light must expand flow outward from within these communities. This also requires that reserves receive literal (i.e., physical), jurisdictional, and metaphysical measures of water, space, and light to facilitate their growth. Only then will indigenous peoples be empowered to make healthier choices about when to live on the reserve, and when to make their life elsewhere.

At the same time as we recognize the fluid boundaries between traditional territories and the reserve, we should recognize that there is a stinginess Anishinaabe peoples exhibit in their love for the land, even as we desire healthier flows. You will remember that zaagi'idiwin has this connotation. This principle directs people to conserve and protect their base, to prevent its waste and dissipation. In particular, Anishinaabe people should be able to fully treat reserves as their own. They demand exclusivity with this partner consistent with the stinginess embodied by zaagi'idiwin.

Nevertheless, exclusivity in the larger sphere will never be the main focus of indigenous peoples' relationships. Over 50 percent of indigenous peoples live off reserves. Over 50 percent marry non-indigenous peoples. Most travel back and forth between cities and reserves during their lifetimes.[82] Indigenous peoples move to the cities to acquire education, get a job, invest in the economy, and buy a house.[83] In so doing, they raise their standard of living. Laws could be designed to encourage this aspect of self-determination while simultaneously ensuring that some of these benefits flow back to the reserves, through noncompulsory means. Likewise, many indigenous peoples leave the cities for the reserve. They do this to learn more about their lands, languages, cultures, and traditions. They want to live closer to their grandparents, parents, aunts, uncles, cousins, and friends. They take up jobs as teachers, administrators, entrepreneurs, and wage laborers. They occupy, develop, and conserve lands. While life on reserves can be socially and culturally rich, in moving to them, these people often sacrifice their material standard of living. Too many fall into poverty. At the same time, lawyers, MBAs, and people with PhDs are among their ranks. They have demonstrated skills. They desperately seek work, but reserves are economically starved, even when surrounded by prosperous cities or aside Canada's most lucrative developments.

No legal or policy instrument will ever be successful in addressing indigenous issues if it does not fully recognize and affirm indigenous people's love for their reserves and territories. This is why self-determination is so important in Canadian law. It is one reason why the Indian Act and our current legal framework is a failure. Our laws do not harness self-determination; they do not incorporate indigenous legal principles like zaagi'idiwin, zaagiin, zaagi'bagaa, zaagajiiwegaaba, and zhawenim.

---

82. John Borrows, "Physical Philosophy: Mobility and the Future of Indigenous Rights," in *Indigenous Peoples and the Law: Comparative and Critical Perspectives*, ed. Shin Imai, Kent McNeil and Ben Richardson (Hart Publishing: Oxford, 2009).

83. Evelyn Peters and Chris Andersen, eds., *Indigenous in the City: Contemporary Identities and Cultural Innovation* (Vancouver: University of British Columbia Press, 2013).

It is clear that my arguments involve a vigorous defense of Indian reserves and their relationship with our larger traditional territories. I want to defend Indian reserves, since I believe too few politicians, academics, and newspaper columnists make this case. In fact, if anything, it seems as if most take the opposite approach—they run down our homelands. In my eyes, it seems as if most opinion leaders deride the places indigenous peoples love the most. Of course, there is a lot to critique, and such analysis must be crisp, loud, and clear. I never want to shy away from addressing the serious problems found on reserves. At the same time, such evaluations must be balanced. They must take into account how a great many indigenous people feel about their reserves and larger traditional territories. They love them. They would and do die for them. When they choose to stay on a reserve or move back to one, they statistically shorten their life span. Yet they move anyway because, despite all the challenges, there is love at home. Reserves are a font of family life, language, culture, sustenance, tradition, social belonging, and meaning for many indigenous peoples. I think the general public is often misled into thinking that Indian reserves are unremitting sources of unfailing misery because of this lack of a vigorous defense of reserves. This is not the case; reserves are complex spaces which also contain humor, mutual aid, and deep spiritual and physical connectedness.

I hope what I am saying is heard in a balanced way. While I am celebrating the absolute centrality of reserves to many indigenous peoples, I must reiterate that I strongly raise my voice against the poverty, violence, and lack of opportunity found within them. I also deplore the lateral violence circulating between and among indigenous peoples on too many reserves. Despite these challenges, instead of getting rid of them I want to see them strengthened, so love can flow more freely in and out of them. This is why we need a stronger recognition and affirmation of indigenous law.

Our love for our territories and reserves might explain why some strongly resist the deep geological internment of nuclear waste in our soils on the shores of Lake Huron.[84] Other communities may resist pipelines, fracking, unsustainable tar sands development, open pit mining, deforestation, and other changes to the land for similar reasons.[85] We love these lands. We know other Canadians do too. This is why they also resist the land's destruction.[86] We must find better ways to express and enhance our mutual love. Of course, we need oil, wood, or minerals for warmth, shelter, transportation, and other commercial activity. While these resources must be used more responsibly, lovingly, and sustainably, they can be used to make a better life for those we love. At the same time, too many resources are developed, priced, distributed, and used in devastating ways. We cannot indiscriminately destroy our natural environment without also destroying what and whom we love.[87]

84. For an introduction to some of the principles on which this opposition is based, see Deborah McGregor, "Traditional Knowledge and Water Governance: The Ethic of Responsibility," *AlterNative: An International Journal of Indigenous Peoples* 5 (2014), 493.

85. Makere Stewart-Harawira, "Returning the Sacred: Indigenous Ontologies in Perilous Times," in *Radical Human Ecology: Intercultural and Indigenous Approaches*, ed. Lewis Williams, Rose Alene Roberts, Alastair McIntosh (Burlington, VT: Ashgate, 2012), 73.

86. For a variety of perspectives on this issue, see Silver Donald Cameron, *The Green Interview*, at http://www.thegreeninterview.com/. In these interviews I discuss how I treasure the peace, friendship, and respect which law can facilitate. I am pro law and order. For me, when lands or waters are polluted or destroyed, this represents the destruction of an important legal archive. Whenever an ecosystem goes silent, a meaningful law is erased. Anishinaabe law is observed in the waters, written on the earth, and reflected in the sky—as long as the rivers flow, the grass grows, and the sun shines. Since Canada's highest laws also incorporate these sources where aboriginal and treaty rights are concerned, any destruction of these energies also diminishes our collective constitution.

87. Some people in the world go to war over their borders being transgressed and their resources stolen. While indigenous peoples have stood on blockades and occupied public thoroughfares and other sites to protect what they love, they still do so through love. Amazingly, we see little violence. We should probably expect no less than civil disobedience when indigenous peoples find that who and what they love is threatened or diminished in significant ways.

Of course, when I speak about these concepts in reference to Indian reserves and traditional territories I am romanticizing a little. That's what we do when we are in love. I think we need to be more romantic in expressing our love for one another and our lands. At the same time, I am keenly aware that romantic love should not blind us to the needs of others.[88] We should not get carried away by this emotion and forget our other values and needs. Nationalism or other forms of self-interest can be destructive forces if not tempered with a love of others, whoever they are and wherever they may live. This includes the love I am discussing in this chapter. While I believe Anishinaabe law encourages this tempering and respect—as does Canadian law more generally—it is also imperfect. Both love and law are incomplete without action and development in relationship with others. We must join our best legal insights to help one another avoid the misery, pain, and destruction all societies face when love fails to guide their actions.

When I worked with Judge David Arnott in the Office of the Treaty Commission for Saskatchewan, we frequently heard about the power of love to positively affect the relationship between the Crown and indigenous people. For example, Elder Simon Kytwayhat of the Makwa Sahgeihcan First Nation, Treaty 6, related a thought-provoking story that placed loved at the center of Canada's treaty relationships. His story, which I have heard in other places, unfolds as follows:

> A long time ago they put a human being in this world. . . . the Creator, he ask the animals, he ask them to come in the circle and he ask there's going to be a two-legged people coming in this

88. I also know Canadians have conflicting loves. Some of us love money more than the lands and waters from which it is made.

earth and there's something special I've got for those people, but where can I put it? Then the grizzly bear spoke, "I will take it to the mountains and I will hide it over there." "No, they're going to find it and they're going to misuse it." Then the big fish, kinosew, he said, "I will take it and I will hide it at the bottom of the ocean." Then again the Creator said, "They're going to find it and they're going to misuse it." Then the buffalo spoke, he said, "I will take it to the berries and I will hide it over there." "No, the people they're going to find it over there and they're going to misuse it." Then the eagle said, "I will take it to the moon, they can't go there." "No, they're going to go there and they're going to misuse it." The little mole came out from under the ground, he said, "Creator, let me hide it, let me hide it some place." Then these big animals were saying "shush." You know, sometimes we don't listen to our people when they want to speak and maybe they got the answer. And the Creator told the big animals, he said, "Let's listen to him." So they listened to him, "Why don't you hide it here for those people? When they found it they won't misuse it."

The Elder Kywayhat concluded with the principle underlying the story. He said:

You know, when we found that love there, and justice, and also how to work together, also how to relate to each other as a brother and sister, I think that's the way the Elders, when they sign that treaty, that's the way they would look at it.[89]

89. Elder Simon Kytwayhat, Treaty Elders of Saskatchewan, Office of the Treaty Commissioner, December 2001, Justice Symposium, transcript, at page 100. Elder Kytwayhat continued:

When the Queen Victoria was saying to people, Indian people, I will give you my children to look after you. I will give you one person to look after your animals, and

CONCLUSION: THE END?

They All Lived … Happily Ever After? Or …
Love Is Lost, and Everyone Dies at the Story's End?

Now that I have walked through my argument, we return to our story at the beginning of this essay. I must say—this is not the end. We can't be really sure if our protagonists will regain their true love. We don't know if they will live happily ever after. Like most complex dramas, the ending will probably be both more banal and complex. The explicit injection of love into law (it is already implicitly there is many instances) makes me exceedingly uncomfortable. I am terrified about its scope and power for causing harm. Both law and love can be discomforting and provoke fear, even as they can be great sources of comfort and affirmation. Love can be a tremendously destructive force. Thus, if we tell ourselves this story ends in everlasting peace and reconciliation, the story would be too trite. It would be hollow, and not reflect the real world. A happy ending here might boost our spirits, and make us feel good, but deep down we would likely be dissatisfied. Fiction, like most good literature, must be true for us to fully embrace it.

Most of our best stories have a snake in the garden or place a trickster in our midst. Our best stories mingle good and bad; there

also I will give you a doctor to look after you when you are sick. And also Indian Affairs. And also I will give you the RCMP to look after you, to protect you. This is what we need to understand in our circle. This is what I like to see the government to understand because we're walking on the treaty every day on the Mother Earth. And the life we have, the grandfather sent, he's the one give us the life. And they're still going in the circle. Our treaty is very strong in the water, in our body, the river. This is what I like to see the government to understand.

Elder Kytwayhat told the gathering that his boss at Joe Duquette High School had passed the story along to him. His boss in turn, similarly followed this set of rules by indicating that he heard the story from his ancestors, his *kohkom*.

is happiness to a degree, but there is also a lingering sense of tension. Of course, a story's resolution falls along a spectrum. Some end with a greater degree of success, while others end with only a sliver of hope. I have much more than a sliver of hope. I believe Canadian law is slowly incorporating indigenous principles in our national rights narrative. I am encouraged, despite the sharp harshness of our colonial winter.

But, I am not the only author of this story. In fact, I am a very minor character. Prime ministers, Supreme Court justices, editorial boards, and corporate officers spill most of the blood and ink in this drama. Fortunately, we also live in a democracy; all of us have some small influence over this script, at least theoretically. What kind of authors will we be? How will we practice customary law in our interactions as indigenous and non-indigenous people? How will we see this theme even more broadly in our societies, when working beyond the indigenous sphere? What will our judges and politicians say about the role of indigenous law in writing section 35(1)'s story? Will they see this is a love story?

Perhaps it's best to conclude, for now, with John Milton:

> So law appears imperfect, and but given
> With purpose to resign them, in full time,
> Up to a better covenant, disciplined
> From shadowy types to truth; from flesh to spirit
> From imposition of strict laws to free.[90]

---

90. John Milton, *Paradise Lost and Other Poems* (New York: Mentor Books, 1961), bk. 12, lines 300–304.

Chapter 6

Legal Challenges in a Changing World

HELENA KENNEDY

It is a great honor to be invited to the extraordinary Canadian Museum for Human Rights to give this lecture. It was Kofi Annan who said that human rights are a yardstick by which we measure human progress. But if history has taught us anything, it is that the march is not always onward and upward; our freedoms are indeed fragile. New events: revolutions, wars, pandemics, environmental crises, natural disasters, disputes over land, fears over security—all can lead to repressive and inhumane outcomes. Change, if not managed with care, can lead to high levels of anxiety, which in turn feed the flames of authoritarianism and oppression.

The world has changed in extraordinary ways in my adult life. My children used to laugh and ask me to tell them about the olden days, if I casually remarked on the world as it was: a world without Google and the internet, a world with very little exotic travel, a world where mothers did not work outside the home and where the work they did, inside the home, was so labor intensive. Yes, this was the world from which I reached adulthood. Tracking the journey we have made in my lifetime still amazes me, but we do not have to go back that far. Just in the last thirty years we have seen the fall of the Berlin Wall and the end of communism throughout Eastern Europe and the former Soviet Union. We have seen the end of totalitarianism in many other parts of the world. The number of democracies has grown exponentially. I spent many of my student weekends demonstrating against Apartheid in South Africa and picketing the Chilean and other Latin American embassies, denouncing their dictators. And then, miraculously, places like South Africa and Latin America managed to shed their old regimes and rid themselves of tyranny. Increasingly the Arab nations are facing tumult as their people demand freedom too. The human yearning for freedom inevitably drives the desire for democracy, albeit not always on the Westminster model. The right to choose those who will govern us is a profound expression of freedom; it is about freedom of choice of a people.

Market philosophy has spread across the world, and not just the idea of markets but *turbocharged* free markets, sometimes with great benefits, but sometimes decidedly not, with places like Russia taking to the new order with so much relish that a kleptocracy now runs the show, crime is rampant, and people live close to the breadline, scrimping to pay privately for education and healthcare. We have seen a shocking growth in the numbers of the super-rich around the globe so that the richest 1 percent in the world now own more than the poorest three billion of the earth's residents. And these huge gaps in wealth are also seen closer to home. Today, the CEO of a top company in the United States earns 325 times the wage of the average worker. In 1980, it was forty-two times the average wage. So the gap between ordinary people and the boss is now like the grand canyon. Some feel our developed democracies have fallen into the hands of a plutocracy, a rich few who control the political strings, with inadequate restraint upon their powers.

In this same period we have seen a withering of trade unions. The power of trade unions to aggregate the interests of workers as distinct from their employers—an important aspect of any fair workplace—has diminished and it is mainly the public sector that is unionized. We have seen a huge growth in the power of lobbyists, pushing their clients' interests on government departments and politicians. Consequentially, politics in Western democracies has taken on a vanilla flavor where parties sing too often from the same hymn sheet with the unholy words written by PR firms, and they are all about pushing markets into every aspect of our lives. Some vested interests have become too great to challenge. We Scots like to think we invented capitalism. Certainly Adam Smith, the famous Scot, expounded brilliantly on the power of market forces in his treatise *The Wealth of Nations*. I myself have paddled in these waters on BBC radio, positing that markets thrived particularly well in common-law countries because of the flexibility of the common law. However, the piece of Adam Smith's theory that is currently forgotten is contained in his book *The Theory of Moral Sentiments*. There, he emphasizes the vital role of ethics in successful markets and the responsibilities owed by capitalists to the community at large. We hear less of ethics in contemporary debates. Even international organizations like the International Monetary Fund and the World Bank have drunk the Kool-Aid and signed up for a wholesale privatization agenda, which means that even in arid parts of Africa, water is owned by profit-making companies.

But the good stuff in our lives cannot be minimized. The changes in women's lives in the West have been revolutionary. There was a time when we had to remind people that women's rights were also human rights. Of course there are battles still to be won, but when I qualified as a lawyer in the 1970s, we had no sex discrimination or equal pay act.

Women were a novelty in professions other than teaching and nursing, and we were still seen as a liability in the workplace because we were likely to go off and have babies. The ability to control our reproduction meant that women suddenly were freed from the fear of frequent pregnancies. Upon the arrival of antidiscriminatory laws, chambers and law firms then openly said they did not take women. Then they said, "Women? We've got one."

Now our universities have half women and sometimes more. And while the workplace is still not completely woman friendly, for the most part, it has changed beyond recognition.

The gains in civil rights for women and racial minorities have been awesome. Who would have thought back in the 1970s that the United States of America, the nation with a desperate history of slavery and Jim Crow laws and Black Panther insurrection, would have a black president by 2009. And the battles around race and gender have led to another enormous shift—gay rights, whereby people are increasingly free to live and love openly, irrespective of their sexuality. On many of these issues, Canada has led the way. Your Charter of Rights and your enlightened judiciary became a lodestone for lawyers like me back in the United Kingdom. It was to Canadian case law that we turned for precedent on domestic violence and rape and many rights issues concerning minorities. We may have brought you the common law, but the gifts came back multifold. Your visionary engagement with human rights was a source from which we drew sustenance.

These gains for women have not been limited to the West. Women in other parts of the world have also been pursuing their own routes to freedom and equality, but it is that much harder to pursue women's rights when extreme poverty is a major blight in your life and daily survival is your primary challenge. Women often remain hampered by the heavy weight of religious and cultural hegemony. Patriarchal control is hard to shed, as we know from our own history. The great change in women's lot comes about when women have educational opportunities and then demand access to power for themselves. But I will return to the fragility of women's gains later.

We have seen extraordinary technological advances, which cannot be underestimated. They have altered how we communicate beyond all imagining. Human relationships are changing as a result. We are able to relate to people and do business across the globe with the pressing of keys. Privacy is fast disappearing. The arrival of the digital age is also shaking to their foundations industries and services which have been mainstays of our nations for eons—newspapers, old-fashioned postal services, publishing, television companies, the music industry, and libraries. The internet may be killing the main streets of our towns because people are buying online, yet that opportunity is a godsend to the time-scarce worker or the country dweller located far from the mall. Sourcing materials and suppliers and opening up trading relationships with people on the other edge of the earth are now daily occurrences.

Connectivity has, like most advances, brought bonuses but also minuses. There is a welter of content with few compasses to guide us through it. There is a slew of opinion and a flood of pornography. There is hacking and whistleblowing and information gathering about all of us on a scale that could never have been foreseen, but there is also an extraordinary world of knowledge at our fingertips— whoever we are. Learning is no longer a privilege. I used to fear there would be a huge technological divide between rich and poor, but go to Africa and you will see the cell phone everywhere: women coffee growers are able to do business with their mobile; women organizing for land reform chivvy politicians by phone.

But law often does not know where to begin in dealing with infringement and lawlessness within this new landscape. We are actually in the middle of a revolution as powerful as the Industrial Revolution. Globalization is the name we give it. And just as the Industrial Revolution presented us with the need for new laws—the nineteenth century was an incredible era for law reform: women received property rights and gained the ability to divorce; laws were configured to protect contracts but also to protect industrial laborers, machinists, and factory workers, as well as to prevent child exploitation. Now we are going to need new law for these new twenty-first-century circumstances.

Law has to be at the heart of social change. You need a system of law and regulation or chaos reigns. We often describe law as one of the twin pillars (with democracy) needed for a civilized society. Without it nothing works. But it too must be a key component of globalization. So what kind of law? How can we create a web of law that is enabling and not disabling of economic progress and well-being but which prevents abuse and exploitation and instils safeguards for human rights?

Ease of travel, telecommunications, the internet, the web and cell phones, the electronic transfer of money: all these factors have expanded markets and also made possible the free movement of people and of ideas. Television bounces images into even the humblest of homes, showing how the other half lives, raising people's hopes for different and better lives. Our world has shrunk. We are living in more connected ways than ever before. Law is rooted in our nations' histories, but increasingly we are having to find ways of expanding law's reach beyond borders.

Globalization is presenting our world with a whole set of new challenges. As markets have opened up so too has the opportunity for black markets in drugs, arms, human labor, and human body parts. Just as there are international corporations doing business across borders, so too there are international crime syndicates working in precisely the same way using all the same mechanisms, including offshore accounts and the banking system. And terrorist organizations use the same model—electronic transfers of money, cell phone contact, encrypted email, and so on.

We have seen a huge growth in the trafficking of women and children for sexual purposes. A UK report last week showed that a quarter of trafficked victims in Britain are children. There is also the serious issue of migrant laborers being used to get around minimum wage standards. I have just led an inquiry in Scotland for the Equality and Human Rights Commission into Human Trafficking, and the evidence was soul destroying—a catalogue of misery. And it is all about the pursuit of profit. Sometimes the boundaries between what is legitimate and illegitimate pursuit are very hazy indeed. Land owners and business people subcontract the provision of labor to gangmasters who bring in the migrants to live in appalling conditions while claiming publicly that such workers are self-employed and outside their responsibility.

Domestic servitude has also risen above the radar, a neighborhood presence of which we had been totally ignorant. People brought from back home in Bangladesh or Pakistan, or from the Philippines or parts of Africa, who sleep on mats on the kitchen floor, have their passports removed, work from dawn until past midnight, and see no money because the employer pays a pittance to the family back in some rural village. Human trafficking is a human rights issue, but it becomes muddled up with illegal immigration, and the people who suffer are those who are the victims—often bundled back home to be retrafficked. So terrified of their traffickers and the threat not just to themselves but also their families that they remain silent unless good systems are in place to provide sanctuary and support. Yet certainly in the United Kingdom, political anxieties over immigration mean that border agencies operate a culture of disbelief when people claim asylum or trafficking, and even those brave enough to tell their stories are met with a wall of suspicion.

In handling international crime, defeating terrorism, addressing climate change, dealing with the issues of migration and asylum, and tackling human trafficking we have to create common international standards. And indeed we do make treaties and create protocols on all these issues, but when we try to bind people together into shared modalities instead of raising standards, standards are too often driven down.

A good example is international terrorism. It has become an urgent problem. In the United Kingdom, four years after 9/11, we had our own horror, albeit on a smaller scale. The 7/7 suicide bombs across London's transport network killed fifty-five people and maimed or hurt hundreds more. That was in 2005. Tony Blair, our then Prime Minister, demanded that the rules of the game had to change, by which he meant that we had to think again about basic principles like habeas corpus, the standard of proof, the right to jury trial, and the presumption of innocence. He wanted the power to lock people up for ninety days without charge. Happily, blood pressure returned more or less to normal and the House of Lords stopped some of this encroachment. However, terrorist events like this can inevitably lead politicians into populist rhetoric and reductions in rights. When fearful citizens sign a blank cheque, as it were, legal principles—which have been carefully constructed over centuries—are suddenly surrendered. We have our Supreme Court to thank for preserving some important standards. After 9/11, the United Kingdom introduced indefinite detention without trial for aliens, which our judges declared contrary to human rights. The use in our courts of intelligence from countries where torture is endemic was also declared contrary to human rights. However, we have introduced secret courts. They started to deal with deportations of persons deemed a threat to national security so that sensitive evidence can be heard without disclosure to the accused. Both the accused and his lawyer are excluded from the court when such evidence is given, but a special advocate with a security clearance is appointed to hear the evidence and test it. The problem remains that this special advocate is not allowed to speak to the detainee, so possible defenses or challenges to the evidence are highly unlikely. We know that changes introduced in times of emergency have a nasty way of leeching into the system and remaining in force long after the crisis, as well as spreading into areas far beyond that for which they were originally sought. We now have British people who suffered rendition to places where they were tortured, ending up finally in Guantanamo Bay, and who allege that our intelligence services were not only privy to what happened but complicit in having their civil action held in secret courts too. Inquest hearings may also be heard in secret. The risk attached to secrecy is that it is used to cover government misbehavior. The cleansing light of day is not shone into dark places.

Our freedoms are fragile and claims upon them made for the protection of national security, and where we can never imagine the shifts impacting on OUR lives, are often the very ones we have to watch carefully. A little bit of this and a little bit of that can lead to detriments we had never imagined. It is called the law of unintended consequences.

We in the United Kingdom had the experience of terrorism back in the 1970s and 1980s, and I was involved in many of the leading cases from the Brighton bombing trial to the Guildford 4 appeal. These experiences taught me that emergency laws cannot be vacuum sealed like something bought in the supermarket. When we lower standards for terrorism, we change the legal culture and it impacts inevitably on other areas of our law. We suffered the consequences for years with an impunity felt by police to force people into confessions and doctor evidence not just in terrorism cases but in all areas of crime. Miscarriages of justice destroy trust in the system, and it takes years to rebuild it. I thought we had learned, but unfortunately we never do.

The globalizing of crime and other threats creates a need for unified responses across nations. So the idea of legal processes with shared norms that cross borders seems eminently sensible. And yet none of it is easy. Creating international systems involves some surrender of sovereignty and nations are torn apart with divisions over how much power international courts should have. It is why the United States will not recognize the International Criminal Court, and it is why we in the United Kingdom are seeing campaigns from the political Right to withdraw from the European Court of Human Rights. Yet without international systems to set standards and bring criminals to book, how do we proceed?

This was a problem Eleanor Roosevelt grappled with after World War II when she sat down with others and asked: How can we prevent another Holocaust? The parliament (the Bundestag) of Germany, which was democratically elected, passed laws which were then administered by the courts. Judges and lawyers sought to justify their part in the annihilation of the Jews by saying, "I was only following the law." Surely the rule of law had to mean more than just passing laws by a majority and then administering them.

However, what Roosevelt recognized was that law comes out of the rich soil of a nation's culture and traditions. While common-law countries like Britain, the United States, Canada, and Australia believed in creating law by developing precedent and using juries, many other countries did things very differently. Eleanor Roosevelt realized that it would be too interventionist and controversial to try to create one system of law for all nations. What the Universal Declaration of Human Rights created was a template of values against which all systems of law could be tested. By sitting down together with representatives of many nations with all perspectives, religious and ideological, she sought to identify the values that are common to all cultures. It then became the duty of signatory nations to make their own domestic laws conform to the declaration.

We in Europe have done that through the European Convention on Human Rights (ECHR). We were not just signatories; we actually drafted it—indeed it was eminent conservative politicians and lawyers who drafted it. There was a touch of the old British condescension involved, of course, with us imagining that it was really the other nations of Europe who needed it—not us—so it took many years before we actually embedded it into our domestic law. Prior to 1998, we could not invoke our rights under the ECHR in our own courts: we had to wait till we had exhausted our domestic remedies and then argue our convention rights in Strasbourg. Since the passing into law of the Human Rights Act of 1998 and the Scotland Act 1998 we have incorporated the *European Convention* into UK law and it has undoubtedly impacted on our legal culture in significant ways—not to the liking of the tabloid press or the tea party tendencies within our polity who do not like things foreign and who see an erosion of British parliamentary sovereignty in our engagement with the European court.

They argue that no foreign court should tell us what to do. They know that arguing against human rights per se would be to paint themselves in ugly colors, so they insist that they support human rights but that the court has departed from the original purpose of the convention—to stop egregious abuses of human rights. But, they say, it was never the intention of the drafters to prevent nations from deporting immigrants to places where there may be tortured. Nor could the drafters have meant that the United Kingdom cannot send back, from whence they came, people convicted of crime even if they now have a family here in the UK and have established deep roots. They accuse the judges in Europe and even our own judges of judicial activism of a liberal kind. We have moved into Justice Scalia territory—he of the US Supreme Court who communes with the American Founding Fathers as to the meaning of the Constitution. The idea that the Human Rights Convention should be a living breathing document which reflects our times with due deference to national customs and practices is not their view. They want the European court to back off. It is right to say that the court, like all courts, sometimes gets it wrong, but being part of an international fabric which sets standards for many nations has crucial value in a world going through convulsive change. President Putin of Russia would love to see the United Kingdom renegotiate its relationship with the European court so that it could pick and choose which judgments to follow. He would vote for that. As a fellow member of the Council of Europe he would be all too happy to have a democratic override like the one being advocated by British conservatives, so that he could merrily ignore the European court's strictures on his locking up journalists and political opponents.

Environmental challenges and climate change are also international and need the establishment of norms that bind us all. Global warming and extreme weather are not going to solved by a one-nation King Canute. The rich parts of the world have developed lifestyles—the car, central heating, air-conditioning, foreign travel in jumbo jets—which are making huge demands on the world's resources, bringing consequent problems for the environment. Upcoming nations want all the same things—cars and high-functioning homes—so the pressure on the ecology of our globe is huge. Individual nations cannot alone confront the issue of global warming. Some recognize the need for international agreements and rules about consumption, but the consequent tensions are tangible. The developed world wants to give up nothing, and the developing world says, "Well, we want our turn at all the good stuff." The corporates have their own vested interests at stake. Global standards would make it very difficult to move your operation to a place where controls are nonexistent.

There are increasing calls for an international environment court or an extension of the jurisdiction of the International Court of Justice to include climate change and environmental degradation and its consequences for the human rights of people around the world. It seems to me that we should certainly be looking at the creation of a model statute on climate change justice which, like the Universal Declaration of Human Rights, creates a framework of standards to which all nations would be expected to sign up. Crimes against humanity and war crimes now exist within a framework of global jurisdiction—these crimes can be prosecuted anywhere, not just where they were committed. That conceptual model should be extended to crimes against the environment. What is needed is some consistency globally on issues of causation and liability.

We may have seen, please God, the end of world war, but conflicts across the world are shockingly prevalent. It is likely that scarcity will create an increasing number of resource wars—wars where the real issue of contention is access to oil, gold, diamonds, uranium, and even water (.e.g., Iraq, Congo, Middle East). It also seems that in response to the uncertainties of globalization, people seek certainty in the politics of identity, which leads to ethnic conflict (Bosnia, Rwanda, Darfur, Chechnya, the Sudan).

Most of the world agrees that there should be clear international law about when a war is a just war. Self-defense has always been a legitimate reason to go to war. It has been accepted since the development of the nation-state that one state has no business interfering with the autonomy of another, that we must respect a nation's right to conduct its internal affairs as it wishes. However, many in the developed world want clearer rules as to when there should be humanitarian intervention. Syria has thrown this into stark relief. Outsiders ask themselves whether it is right to stand by while genocides or crimes against humanity are taking place inside another nation. What would dwellers in the twenty-first century do in the face of Hitler's attempt to exterminate the Jews? Do we not need clearer international rules about our collective responsibilities? Do the vetoing rules of the Security Council deliver justice? I am satisfied that they do not. For reasons of their own, China and Russia vote against any intervention. Now I am not here seeking to legitimize the invasion of Iraq, where the coalition of the willing failed to comply with international law. There was no self-defense—although we saw the doctoring of intelligence to make it seem that we were all under immediate threat from Saddam Hussein. There was no harboring of al-Qaeda terrorists. There were no weapons of mass destruction. We had stood idly by when he was engaged in the mass killing of his citizens, so sudden concern for the people of Iraq seemed suspect. So the situation did not conform to international law. But I have no doubt that it was misuse of international powers in Iraq that prevented action in Syria. Our publics have lost confidence in our adherence to legal principle. That is what happens when law is misused; trust is lost.

Human rights abuses around the world are not diminishing and we in the developed world have to bear some responsibility. Torture, extrajudicial killings, rendition, disappearances—too many governments take a very loose view of the rule of law and commit what can only be described as state terrorism against their own people. We in the West turn a blind eye to such conduct in nations, which for strategic or other self-interested reasons, we call our allies. Trading is a higher priority, and we console ourselves that we cannot solve the world's problems. But an injection of ethics would be a good thing here too. What is needed is some global leadership.

We also know that with all the other inequalities that exist, women all over the world still bear additional burdens. They face special forms of inequality, inhumanity, and persecution: rape, domestic violence, forced marriage, child marriage, female genital mutilation, widow burning, honor killings, enforced prostitution, unequal pay, denial of education, and trafficking. The list is long but unfortunately many of these practices are sanctioned by the communities in which they are practiced. Can communities which have different cultures be expected to comply with international standards? I have taken part in countless debates over the years about cultural relativism and the West imposing its values on the rest of the world, but I hold firmly to the view that there are some values which are universal and the right not to face physical harm is one of those. However, great pressure is often applied to the whole international human rights framework to leave cultural practices alone. The argument is made that women in such cultures adhere to the teaching freely.

Cultural relativism refers to the view that all cultures are equal, and universal values become secondary when examining cultural norms. This being so, no outside value should automatically be deemed superior to that of the local culture. For example, if the local culture allows female circumcision or genital mutilation (FGM), then the human right prohibiting cruel or degrading treatment should not prevent the cutting of the clitoris or the labia. If the culture accepts it, then no outside human rights principle should overrule the cultural norm. The same would be true of women and girls being forcibly veiled in some Muslim countries under threat of imprisonment or lashes. Strict cultural relativists would say that is about religious respect and not a matter of human rights being abused.

One problem with cultural relativism is that it avoids examining the very societal structures that create the cultural norm in the first place. Who determines culture? He who decides controls the outcome, and it usually is "he." The power to define culture, the power to determine religious and legal norms has rested with men. And not just any men but the leading male power sources within societies. That is why we should be very careful about leaping to an acceptance of cruel practices without asking what their purpose is or was. The insistence that human rights cannot be universal is often actually about something else altogether—sustaining structures of power that are authoritarian or patriarchal. As Michael Ignatieff has said, "relativism is the invariable alibi of tyranny."

A few years ago, the British Court of Appeal and subsequently the House of Lords heard a woman's case for asylum based on her facing enforced FGM on return to Sierra Leone. FGM is justified as keeping women chaste, proving virginity on marriage, and making women more restrained. Part of the legal debate turned on the acceptance of the practice by women (not men) in the community as though endorsement of abuse by those who had hitherto been abused made it alright. For example, the judges asked: Is it persecution of "women as a particular social group" when so many women accepted it as a practice?

When I travel on human rights work, I do not find sweeping resistance to human rights. In fact, it is usually *governments* who do not like human rights discourse because it shines a light on their conduct, or it is male elders in communities who insist on preserving culture and tradition.

In some societies it is argued that it is right for men to have power over women: strictly controlling whom women can marry, whom they can talk to, and where they are allowed to go. I met a young Somalian woman recently who told me that equality for women was contrary to her religion—Islam. Of course, many Muslims would explain that this is nonsense and a corrupted interpretation of the holy book, but many women are taught this view. It is not that long ago that women in the West thought that politics was the business of men and many argued against having the vote. People do argue against their own interests. I still find it hard to understand so many blue-collar workers voting Republican in the United States. But the point of human rights is not to say people cannot live in a way of their choosing. Human rights do not seek to prevent people living life in their communities as they want. The point is that the individuals should be *free* to choose whether they wish to live a life according to those principles. There has to be the freedom to opt out of such approaches to living without fear of punishment. In a trip to Iraq, I visited a prison with a women's section and women in there were guilty of crimes against morality, typically relationships outside marriage. There were no men in prison for immorality with women.

Making the case for universalism can be particularly difficult in those circumstances where those who are the victims of human rights violations actually condone the culture or community that legitimizes the abuse of their rights. What should not be forgotten is that these individuals will often lack the resources—whether financial, educational, or otherwise—to challenge the diminution of their rights. They may even consent because they simply cannot withstand the pressure not to consent. And perhaps even more key is that the very injustice, which deprives a woman in a deeply patriarchal society of some of her rights, may deny her the ability to even IMAGINE an alternative. Many women accept subjugation because to challenge the status quo is a frightening as well as a liberating prospect.

As well as the position and treatment of women, the issues which inflame most controversy and rejection of human rights are the death penalty, torture, homosexuality, and freedom of expression, with different nations arguing their right to cultural difference rather than bow to any outside principle. Each one of those issues, raged over in other parts of the world, has a blowback effect in Europe—the death penalty limits the United Kingdom's ability to deport, as does the prohibition on torture.

On homosexuality, we now interpret the right to family life as including a partnership with a person of the same sex, which has meant allowing immigrants who have formed committed relationships akin to heterosexual marriage to remain in the United Kingdom. Men and women fleeing persecution because of their sexuality are seeking asylum. On women's rights we have had to confront customs and practices which live on but which we find unacceptable—from child marriage to forced marriage, honor killing, forced prostitution (this is increasingly seen in human trafficking cases)—but again there is a backlash against providing sanctuary and asylum to women fleeing these practices because asylum is conflated with immigration—a toxic electoral issue. Immigration is one of the main reasons why the concept of human rights is so antagonistic to sections of the Right.

So this is altogether a critical time for the assertion of the rule of law and the development of human rights. The shift toward democracy across Eastern Europe, the Middle East, Latin America, Asia, and Africa has put human rights and the rule of law at the top of the agenda. Fragile democracies often have a tenuous hold on the meaning of the rule of law, and their judiciaries have had little experience of what it means to be independent of state interference. Lawyers who might have challenged abuse of state power under totalitarianism have often suffered the consequences, so the very concept of an independent legal profession, with lawyers who will conduct a case without fear or favor, is not usually embedded in their systems.

I returned recently from Iraq where I was the independent assessor of human rights programs set up by the US State Department when the Occupation forces withdrew. The problems are manifest. People who have lived under tyranny take a long time to throw off the learned behaviors that go with oppression. The police, the judges, the lawyers: all still too often operate like bureaucrats rather than protectors of the rule of law. The director of the NGO which was delivering the programs told me that he still felt the grip of fear in his guts when he was approached by a policeman or when he stepped forward at passport control. The heavy hand of the state is still a haunting from the past. Transitioning state functionaries into people who will protect citizens and respect their rights is a tough call. Civil servants come new to the idea of neutrality, never mind civility. In a country at risk of descending totally into sectarian strife between Sunni and Shia Islam, the creation of institutions which will operate free of discriminatory practices is imperative but hard. The concepts of human rights are new and, without courts which will uphold them, can be meaningless. I met wonderful women— the country is full of widows—who had come to realize the importance of state recognition of marriage. Without documentation, many who had been married almost as children by the local Imam had no way of proving their marital status and thus substantiating their claim to a meagre state support for widows. The families of their husbands would also come and reclaim the marital home as belonging to their people rather than the wife and her children. The fragile rights that women had were being eroded by poverty, and there had been an increase in old practices of child marriage and the removal of girls from school on reaching puberty. The women activists were clear that they wanted all this stopped, but apart from lobbying, they had no mechanisms to enforce the law which already prohibits these practices. There are no lawyers to take the cases, no resources, no judges willing to hear.

I recently attended a meeting with leaders from the Arab world—Tunisia, Libya, Yemen, and others—and as the discussions unfolded it became clear that the problem is that there are no state institutions in many of these countries, no civil society organizations with which outside NGOs can partner to help develop human rights. Gaddafi ruled Libya without state institutions—which is what is making nation building well-nigh impossible now. The infrastructure does not exist. And where there are courts they are submerged in corruption, tribal allegiances, or state interference. Women do not do well in any of it.

Human rights abuses destabilize countries because where there is imprisonment without trial, disappearances, torture, or persecution of minorities, there is more likely to be insurrection, conflict, and war. Trading or diplomacy with such countries carries serious risks. Globalization has, therefore, made issues of just law a priority. International corporations and even the large banks are recognizing the importance of stable legal systems. But the message has to be that they too must play their part by following some established ground rules on corporate social responsibility. And I am not talking about charitable giving and support for the arts—all of which is fine. I am talking about their role in reducing carbon emissions, their role in paying a living wage to employees and insisting on the same from those with whom they subcontract. The collapse of the factory in Dacca, Bangladesh, was a signal that cheap clothes in the West have a price in poor countries of the world. Here too, there have to be international norms established and enforced, with institutions such as universities, unions, and the like refusing to invest their endowment funds with those who do not comply with global standards. Mary Robinson has just called for this pressure on companies on the subject of global warming.

While we expect there to be problems establishing rights and freedoms in countries in transition, governments in developed democracies are also struggling to cope with the new issues like privacy and the internet are presenting us with yet more problems about how we can invoke law on matters that cross borders, as the internet clearly does. Issues of state power and surveillance that have arisen from both the War on Terror and technological advances are leading to mad behaviors. People like Julian Assange and Edward Snowden are characterized as terrorists by some and heroes by others. The desire for security can lead to the abandonment of legal principle and well-established safeguards. The recent failure to regulate banks was one thing, but the failure to keep on top of security agencies like the NSA (National Security Agency) and GCHQ (Government Communications Headquarters) and to regulate their activities adequately is another serious problem. One problem on security is that those deemed safe enough to know about secrets are usually too close to those they should be calling to account. They often stem in some way from that world. It was true of banking and is true of the spooks.

Into this mix of challenges and fears is another feature of our times that brings legal difficulty. The idea of the nation is being reclaimed with enthusiasm all over the world; people are seeking the comfort of national and religious identity, retiring into smaller and smaller groupings, exhibiting what the political commentator Michael Ignatief calls "the narcissism of minor difference." This makes it harder to speak the language of internationalism and it makes it easier for opponents of international courts to insist upon retreating behind national borders and insist upon the supremacy of their own laws.

In the absence of other ideologies to provide a sustaining vision of our human purpose and because of the world's uncertainties, we have seen an increasing assertiveness of religions. Religion has replaced politics as a dominant form of identity and "taking offense" is a way of refusing to be passive.

The events of September 11, 2001, and of July 7, 2005, have meant Muslims have been the focus of extensive police and intelligence activity, with a sixteen-fold increase in stop and search, hundreds of arrests (of which few lead to charges of any kind), efforts to recruit informants, and many house raids. In Britain, for example, Home Office ministers have made it clear that the Islamic community will have to accept such targeted policing as a necessary feature of combating terrorism.

Elections have shown that British Muslims are seriously alienated from government and feel understandably beleaguered. The war in Iraq added considerably to their belief that new rules are being created where Muslims are concerned, both nationally and internationally. The community has also been at the receiving end of greatly increased harassment from fellow citizens as well as racist attack.

As an olive branch, an offense of "inciting religious hatred" has been created. The mere existence of such an offense will rarely inhibit ugly displays of xenophobic hostility, but it will make people, particularly comedians and writers, uncertain of the law and fearful about crossing the line. It is yet another erosion of civil liberty.

It is important not to minimize the fact that Muslims are experiencing insult and abuse at a heightened level. Most of it is racism in new clothes. What do you do, I am asked, when a dead Muslim woman lying in the morgue has bacon rashers placed on her body, as happened a couple of years ago in London? I have to point out that this law of inciting religious hatred will not deliver any remedy. What you do is sack the attendant who is responsible. You disgrace him or her publicly, making clear our abhorrence at such defilement. The criminal law is not the only answer to disgraceful conduct. Societies have other sanctions which they can bring to bear.

However, existing anti-racist legislation already covers most insult and offense directed at individuals. Indeed the whole raft of public order legislation already in existence around the use of threatening words and behavior covers the acts and words, which Muslims describe when asked to give examples of what they experience and what they want to prevent. Unfortunately, what Muslims also think the legislation will do is prevent critics of their religion from saying things which are offensive to the word of the Prophet in the Koran or of the Prophet himself. Religious conservatives the world over—and this includes Christian fundamentalists and extreme orthodox Jews—often seek to silence others and to impose on society not merely tolerance of their beliefs but actual acceptance of them. Nothing should make us willing to accept the abuse of the human rights of another, but unfortunately, religious texts are often used to do precisely that. So those tensions between freedom of speech and freedom of religion are repeatedly being played out.

The Home Office creators of the legislation insist that the Act will only outlaw an offense directed at followers of a religion not the tenets of the religion itself. They agree that religion, like any other

ideology, should be tested in the marketplace of ideas and even ridi-
culed. However, what Muslims and others want and believe they are
getting is a blasphemy law such as Christians have. It suits community leaders to encourage this belief because it suggests to their own
people that they have wrung potent concessions from government
and it extends their authority. However, the law will not only leave
minority communities unrequited when it fails to produce their
desired outcomes, but it will also affect the willingness of people to
address the most pernicious aspects of religious practice.

Over the years I have had a close association with many women's
organizations, particularly Southall Black Sisters, a London center
which includes Asian women of Sikh, Muslim, and Hindu back-
grounds, but also many other minority women. They have been
struggling for many years against attempts to silence their voices in
relation to violence against women. They are clear in their opposition to the new law on incitement to religious hatred because it
would support and encourage the culture of intolerance that already
exists in all religions. Challenge has to be offered to religions, particularly over human rights issues affecting women, and they have
no doubt that this law would be used as a weapon to suppress dis-
sent within their communities, particularly crushing those who are
more vulnerable and powerless. They point out that increasingly it
is women who are being silenced. Men in community leadership
positions often try to close down debate about abuses of power.
It happened in the Catholic Church over child abuse and priests
fathering children. And it happens in our Asian communities to
silence accounts of abuse within the family, like forced marriage.

One of the first lessons that all citizens should learn is that ill-
considered laws of this kind often have unintended consequences.
I remember, and I am sure you will too, that feminists in Canada
persuaded the Canadian legislature to introduce censorship laws to

deal with pornography only to find them used against homosexual authors; a radical black feminist, who was accused of stirring up race hatred against white people; and Andrea Dworkin, the feminist anti-porn activist. In Eastern Europe and the former Soviet Union, laws against defamation were used to stifle criticism of the communist regimes. A Polish satirist, Jerzy Urban, was in early 2005 convicted and fined in a Warsaw court for mocking the late pope over his poor health. The law used was normally directed at maintaining international relations. In Turkey, defamation laws were used against Ismail Besikci for exposing human rights abuses of Kurds. In South Africa during apartheid, race hate laws were used against the victims of the state's racist policies. Even Alex Haley's novel "Roots" was banned on the grounds that it would "polarize racial feelings."

As religious intolerance rises, dialogue and democracy are more effective tools for combating hatred than laws designed to silence. But again we are seeing how fragile our rights can be. We must always remember that the liberties which have been hewn into our democracy are there by dint of hard struggle and scalding lessons. My clients have taught me why they matter. Individual pain is the clearest point of entry into understanding the importance of human rights. But we can lose rights in times of change and challenge and recovering them is very hard indeed.

Ultimately, what is needed in our shrinking world are legal commitments we can all share. We need to rein in those who have power and that no longer simply means governments: it means corporations; it means bankers; it means internet providers. So the question remains: Can we really expect citizens of the world to become subject to a set of rules common to them all? Is such an aspiration feasible and, if so, is it right?

The rules of football and other major sports have become universal, enabling nations around the world to participate successfully in cross-cultural activity, sometimes creating more effective links between people than any formal diplomacy. So too, the rules of chess. The postal system of the world works on the basis that whatever the disagreements between countries, there is an international commitment to deliver mail. Everyone abides by the rules, and citizens of Cuba and America can exchange letters, as can those of Burma and the United Kingdom. The rules in relation to commerce had to be universalized in order to create effective trade between countries with a clear understanding of the obligations of contracts and the need for legal systems to enforce them. I know from direct experience of chairing the British Council the way in which your country [Canada] and mine assisted China in creating a commercial law base which would be recognized around the world by potential business partners and would assure market confidence. We sent out lawyers to draft the new commercial laws there and helped train whole cohorts of young Chinese commercial lawyers. Our senior UK judges have recently been involved in creating a new commercial law court in the Arab world based in Qatar founded on common-law principles and UK commercial law. Financial and business institutions have made it clear to the world that a sound base in law is essential for trading. So let us disabuse ourselves of the idea that international norms cannot be created. It is simply a matter of making it clear that this is what is needed. It is about political will.

I know that this involves placing a great deal of faith in law. Law alone cannot deliver justice. It needs tolerance and a serious commitment to pluralism. It means high ideals and aspirations. But we have to remember that sometimes we have to engage in an act of faith. The masons who built the great cathedrals of Europe in the eleventh and twelfth centuries rarely saw the product of their endeavors completed. They carved a beautiful panel here or a fine gargoyle there, but they knew that they were contributing to something exquisite and lasting. And we are doing that too. Law can be prosaic and about deals, but human rights is the place where law becomes poetry. And we all know that poetry is really what life should be about.

Chapter 7

Women and the Struggle for Human Rights

GERMAINE GREER

I stand before you as a liberation feminist, and liberation feminism has not even begun. We may say the same thing about the rights of indigenous peoples. We have only just begun to understand what might be involved. And how hard we have to work not to ride rough-shod over concerns and concepts that we barely understand. We have a lot of growing up to do. And insofar as a Museum of Human Rights might help, I am very pleased to see it. But museums are generally places where we store things that are dead and have lost their social relevance. It is to be hoped that this does not happen here.

I am going to begin by throwing you a challenge. I have always said that I am not an equality feminist: I am not interested in equality; equality is a profoundly conservative aim. It would have men and women living together in a world unchanged. Unless the world changes, it is doomed. We have got to make big changes at what could be described as the very last minute.

In 1791, the French feminist Olympe de Gouges took it upon herself to write a *Déclaration des droits de la femme et de la citoyenne.* The Universal Declaration of Human Rights is descended from the *Déclaration des droits de l'homme et du citoyen* passed by the French National Constituent Assembly in 1789. De Gouges simply parses this, by changing the male words to female. Her version begins:

> Les mères, les filles, les soeurs, représentantes de la nation, demandent d'être constitutées en assemblée nationale. Considérant que l'ignorance, l'oubli ou le mépris des droits de la femme sont les seules causes des malheurs publics et de la corruption des gouvernements ont resolu d'exposer dans une déclaration solemnelle, les droits naturels, inaliénables et sacrés de la femme, afin que cette déclaration, constamment présente à tous les membres du corps social, leur rappelle sans cesse leurs droits et leurs devoirs, afin que les actes du pouvoir des femmes, et ceux du pouvoir des hommes pouvant être à chaque instant comparés avec le but de toute institution politique, en soient plus respectés, afin que les réclamations des citoyennes, fondées désormais sur des principes simples et incontestables, tournent toujours au maintien de la Constitution, des bonnes moeurs, et au bonheur de tous.
>
> 1. La femme naît libre et demeure égale à l'homme en droits. Les distinctions sociales ne peuvent être fondées que sur l'utilité commune.
> 2. Le but de toute association politique est la conservation des droits naturels et imprescriptibles de la Femme et de l'Homme: ces droits sont la liberté, la propriété, la sûreté, et surtout la résistance à l'oppression.

De Gouges's *Déclaration* was a tour de force, a *jeu d'esprit* that by simply feminizing the arguments of the original *Déclaration* made clear that the rights of man really didn't fit women, and their recognition would not necessarily satisfy women's needs.

De Gouges was guillotined two years later. If she were to come on earth again, what would she make of the presumed rights of women as they are understood today? The *Déclaration des droits de l'homme* lists those rights as liberty, property, security, and resistance to oppression. If I look in Wikipedia—which God knows is the source of all modern wisdom—I see that the first right of women is to bodily integrity and autonomy. De Gouges didn't mention either bodily integrity or bodily autonomy.

What should we understand by the right to bodily integrity and autonomy? In the 1970s, women carried banners demanding the right to control their own bodies. But no such right can be said to exist, for individuals of any sex. Your body is in fact not under your control. And if you don't know it when you're twenty, you're certainly going to know it by the time you're seventy-five. The issue is more vexed for women because women may become pregnant, that is, host other human beings inside that bodily integrity, grow them in their wombs and give birth to them. This makes women fundamentally different from men and children.

To say that women are essentially different from men is to utter heresy for which I could be burned at the feminist stake. The fact that women are wombed creatures and that gestation of human beings is what happens there is important if we are to understand the extraordinarily complex system of conflicts that arise for women.

A pregnant woman has her bodily integrity breached by the presence within it of another individual. And she doesn't have sole rights in that individual, because that individual also has a father who has rights in the child. There can be no question of denying the rights of a father in his progeny or the rights of that progeny. The important thing is to understand and to defend the rights of the mothers as outweighing the others—not as eliminating them, but as weighing more. Now this already means that we've got a complex calculation to make.

All Canadian women should revere the name of Shulamith Firestone, founder of Red Stockings and the New York Radical Feminists. She was probably the most intellectually consistent and therefore the most radical of all feminists. She said in her book *The Dialectic of Sex*, published in 1970, that women would never be free as long as gestation took place in the uterus. That fact meant that their freedom was compromised from the outset. Do women want to be free? Do they look forward to a time when fetuses made in the laboratory will be brought to full viability outside the body?

Women have wanted to avoid unwanted pregnancy and to plan their families, but they have never demanded to be released from the childbearing role. The pressure to perfect a technique of in vitro fertilization of the human ovum came not from women but from the research community. And who are they? And why were they so interested? What did they think they were doing? Since then, reproductive technology has proliferated to include genetic screening, embryo transfer, embryo splitting, and whatever else is coming up this week. The pressure within the research community to develop new forms of reproductive technology appears to be relentless. Nowadays if a pregnant woman suffers fatal injury, she is likely to be kept on life support until the fetus comes to term, when it will be delivered by cesarean section and the mother's life support turned off. This becomes problematic if the woman's family objects, but in such a case doctors will usually prevail, the pregnancy will continue, and the child will be born motherless.

What were the fertility technicians trying to prove? The demand for in vitro fertilization did not come from the people who bear the burden of childbearing. It came from the people who do not. So far no animal embryo has been brought to viability outside the uterus. But it is only a matter of time before an artificial womb is developed. Some predict that by the end of this century in vitro gestation will be possible. Young women need to think about this. They need to ask themselves whether they want to continue to undergo pregnancy. If it was possible to grow a child in a controlled environment would women abandon uterine gestation? Would they say they will not do this anymore if they do not have to? If families can be safely grown outside the womb? Motherhood is already being deconstructed by embryo transfer and surrogacy so that a single child can have *three* mothers: a genetic mother, a womb mother, and a legal mother. Which of these three has the lowest status? Recent events have revealed that the mother who agrees to grow a child in her womb as a surrogate mother has fewer rights in the child than the parents who have paid her to carry it.

Women are already opting out of labor by choosing to give birth by cesarean section. The rate has risen to 46 percent in China and to levels of 25 percent and above in many Asian, European, and Latin American countries. Western women are not the only ones who are too posh to push. The rate has increased in the United States to 33 percent of all births in 2012, up from 21 percent in 1996.

This is not simply because women are unwilling to undergo the ordeal of labor. A great deal of the pressure to resort to cesarean section is by way of avoiding possible malpractice suits, that is, to protect doctors. A lot of it is conservative medical practice that's meant to limit not the risk to the patient but the risk to the practitioners. How did this happen? Where were we looking when this happened?

Everybody pays for this in the end. Across Europe there are differences between countries, but you might be surprised to learn what they are. In Italy the cesarean rate is 40 percent, while in the Nordic countries it's 14 percent. We're told that rich women opt for cesarean section to avoid pain but also to preserve their vaginal tone—to keep their vagina in good order. Now you might wonder: What for? Certainly not for giving birth. As far as we can tell, it is meant to enhance the experience of vaginal intercourse, but for whom? Whether the husband or other partner is so aware of the vaginal tone, or whether men are a species of tuning forks is nowhere discussed.

Are we all in flight from uterine gestation? Is there a grassroots movement toward some brave new world where we won't have to go through this anymore? There is plenty of evidence that women are not attached to their uteri, that they don't identify themselves as wombed creatures. A mastectomy is a disaster but a hysterectomy is par for the course. The United States has the highest rate of hysterectomy in the world, but Canada is hot on their heels. By the age of sixty, one-third of American women will have had their wombs removed.

What are the Martians going to think when they come to colonize a devastated earth and find that millions of human women were buried without their wombs? We've got the healthiest women in history. Women have never been so well nourished, they've never been so strong or so big, and yet many are having their wombs taken out. Can these hysterectomies be necessary in such large numbers? How many women are having cesareans? Why are they doing that? When I look for the reasons I'm told rich women who can choose, choose cesareans to avoid pain (which they can avoid without having a cesarean!) and because of the mysterious vaginal tone. What is the priority here?

It's not up to me to decide that.

What is up to women to do is to understand that this is an issue that they need to think about. We need to know whether younger women want to be rescued from carrying babies to term within their own bodies. If they do, then fine. Would the outcome of the removal of pregnancy from women be an improvement in their social status, or the opposite? We don't know. We haven't even considered the question.

When twentieth-century feminists demanded the right to control their own bodies, what they actually meant was the right to reproductive choice: the right to refuse penetrative sex, the right to reject unsafe sex, the right of access to contraceptive technology, the right of access to chemical and surgical abortion, the right to reject invasive procedures, and the right to choose a method of childbirth. I can spin that out for hours because there's a whole lot of other rights in there as well, rights to information, rights to having people tell you what they're doing instead of just doing it—during labor for example. But no such right is enshrined in legislation.

It will be clear that a woman can only exercise those rights if she has sufficient information about, for example, the mode of operation of the vast array of chemical and mechanical contraceptives. At the risk of depressing you all horribly, I must point out that the mode of operation of the condom is the easiest to understand. And it has the added benefit of protecting against sexually transmitted disease. Do women have the right to insist on the use of a condom?

In Chapter 6, you heard from Helena Kennedy, who actually prosecuted a really interesting civil case for damages that was brought by two sex workers who had a client who refused to use a condom. The Crown prosecutor had refused to take the case, which was technically a rape case. And Helena brought the case for the women and won it. I wish I could tell you that as a result everything changed. Nothing changed. There has never been another case like it. In any other situation it would have established a precedent.

One of the questions we have to ask ourselves is this: What do we have to do to establish a precedent? At what age does a woman achieve autonomy? In Britain in 2011 7,400 girls aged fifteen or under—almost too young to be called young women—were given contraceptive injections or implants; 1,700 aged thirteen and fourteen were given subdermal implants, and 800 were given injections. This was to prevent them from becoming pregnant when they had unprotected intercourse. Intercourse with girls of this age is illegal. It is a crime. Why were these women being prepped for such use? What could have been the justification? How did the education system and the guardians of public morality allow such a thing to happen? Did nobody care that these young women were exposed to a risk of disease? Sterilizing disease? To human papilloma virus, for example? To chlamydia? Nobody gave a damn. They were concerned about the shame of teenage pregnancy, which they were prepared to avoid via this extraordinary invasion of the young women's bodily integrity.

Once the schoolgirls had received the injectable and the subdermal implants, they were stuck with them. If they had a bad reaction, it could not be fixed. Apparently the selection of girls to undergo these procedures was made on advice from their teachers. I don't know about you, but when I was at school the people who were at it were the little goody-goody girlies who looked as if butter wouldn't melt in their mouths. We noisy girls were as pure as the driven snow. When such an invasion of the young women's human rights was first mooted, it came from someone from the International Planned Parenthood Federation whom I greatly respected. How could he forget his responsibility to the health of young women so far as to suggest such a draconian solution to the perceived problem of teenage pregnancy? For whose convenience were these young women being rendered infertile? Were their parents consulted? That's one question. The next question is: Should their parents be consulted? Is your children's sexuality your business, or did these young women have a claim to bodily integrity? We haven't confronted any of these issues. Why? Why were they not properly debated? Well it might suggest to you that those issues are not important. They take a back seat. A right to bodily integrity and autonomy may be the first of women's rights, but there's no evidence that they actually enjoy such a right or that they have defined such a right or that they've begun to struggle for it.

Most right-thinking people deplore the practice of female genital cutting as practiced by certain cultural groups in Africa. This is more often referred to as FGM, where M stands for mutilation. (Imagine the furor if circumcision were to be routinely referred to as MGM!) In Britain a doctor who performs the operation is breaking the law. Dr. Dhanuson Dharmasena, a registrar in obstetrics and gynecology at the Whittington hospital in north London, was prosecuted for allegedly carrying out FGM on a patient. In fact the surgeon was carrying out a repair on a woman who had been circumcised and had suffered a tear during childbirth. The decision to charge a hospital doctor over a repair rather than the person responsible for carrying out the mutilation in the first place sparked concern in parts of the medical profession. (The case came to trial in February 2015 and Dharmasena was acquitted.) Dharmasena's prosecution is the first ever under the Female Genital Mutilation Act—a full twenty-nine years after FGM first became illegal in England and Wales. So do we care or don't we?

Why would women perform this operation on their own daughters and granddaughters? One of the most common cosmetic procedures in the United States, especially on Afro-American women, is labiaplasty, surgery to reduce the size of the inner labia. The procedure is touted by allegations that 30 percent of women have "excess genital tissue." These procedures are legal; what we don't know is whether they are rational.

Right here in Winnipeg you can spend money on genital cutting: according to a clinic's online advertising, "designer laser vagi-
noplasty" can enhance vulvar structures, labia majora, mons pubis,
perineum, introitus, and hymen. The most common procedure
is laser reduction labioplasty, which will sculpt the elongated or
unequal labia minora (small inner lips) any way you want. Most
women say that they do not want the small inner lips to project
beyond the large outer lips. Laser reduction labioplasty can also
trim excess prepuce (excess skin along the sides of the clitoris)
and is also called clitoral hood reduction. Women say that they
want the skin to drape neatly over the clitoris. The reduction of
the excess prepuce provides the desired aesthetic enhancement
of the clitoral skin. The majority of women having laser reduction
labioplasty need the reduction of excess prepuce for a complete
aesthetic result. Laser perineoplasty can rejuvenate the relaxed or
aging perineum. It can also enhance sagging labia majora (large
outer lips) and labia minora. Overall, the procedure can provide
"a youthful and aesthetically appealing vulva." Augmentation
labioplasty can provide aesthetically enhanced and youthful labia
majora by removing some of the patient's own fat via liposculpturing and transplanting it into the labia majora. Vulvar lipoplasty can
remove unwanted fat of the mons pubis and upper parts of the labia
majora. Liposculpturing can alleviate any unsightly fatty bulges of
this area and produce an aesthetically pleasing contour. And once
you're happy with all those bits, you can line up for a session of anal
bleaching.

We cannot exercise our right to bodily integrity if we are convinced that our bodies are fundamentally unsatisfactory, if our
insecurities are exploited so that we accept expensive and painful
interventions. If we add to the touting of cosmetic surgery the role
of pornography in promoting hairlessness and the infantilization of

women, we must be aware that women are more alienated from their bodies in the twenty-first century than they were fifty years ago.

At what age do women lose their autonomy? The population of age care homes is 85 percent female, and they are locked in. Incarcerated. They are guilty of no crime.

In the 1960s, feminists worked pretty hard to inform women about their bodies. They set out self-examination groups so that women could see what their and other women's vaginas and cervixes looked like. They figured out methods of ending pregnancy without recourse to the medical profession and health authorities, methods they called "menstrual extraction" and similar names. Their aim was to reclaim the management of women's bodies from the health establishment. And in that they can be said now to have utterly failed.

The medico-legal establishment in the United States moved really quickly to regain control over the management of women's bodies, and the result was the momentous decision in the case of *Roe v. Wade*. This didn't come about because of political action by the women of America. What changed the ground rules was the finding that antiabortion legislation infringed the right to privacy enshrined in the due process clause of the Fourteenth Amendment. No issue of principle was involved. It was a play on words. There was no assertion of women's right to choice. There is still bitter conflict in the Americas and in Canada—I include Canada in the Americas— about the right to terminate a pregnancy. There are those who see it as fundamental to women's self-determination on the one hand and those who see it as the right to commit murder.. All these people have rights. And they all need to learn how to live together. As you know, abortion in Canada is not against the law, but there is an issue of availability that reflects the right of practitioners to refuse to be involved. It isn't good enough to decide that the practitioners who refuse to be involved have got to be punished or prevented or stopped from exercising their own right to liberty of conscience. It's something people have fought for. We should be prepared to defend it even when it's inconvenient.

Laws are not enough; you have to understand the politics; you have to understand the situation. What we witness again and again is women's powerlessness. Women just can't make things happen. Remember what Olympe de Gouges said. It sounded like a throwaway line, that women need an assemblée nationale. What we need is to understand how you combine, how you build up pressure, how you put pressure on a political system. We have no idea. Fifty-one percent of the population can't make anything happen. We can join the existing political system. But if we do that we accept the existing political agenda. We can't actually introduce a whole new agenda. How are we going to make that difference?

We have never dealt with misogyny. And one of the things we didn't understand was that when we began to exert ourselves to push for some sort of a deal, some sort of equality, that there would be a swift and sharp revenge. And we didn't really understand either that it wouldn't be necessarily the misogyny of men, although that remains a huge problem. A much bigger problem was the misogyny of women. Why can't we do what men do? Men study to build effective organizations from the time they're small. They have leaders. They have people being groomed for leadership. They have jokers. They have every kind of status within their boy groups. And they discipline each other to present a solid facade to outsiders while they struggle for supremacy within the group.

All of this is completely unknown to women. We don't know about secret societies and we don't know about accumulation of power. We can't do it. I find it quite extraordinary that even when the story about the abduction of three hundred Nigerian schoolgirls by Boko Haram broke in the Western media in April 2014, it was a month before anybody did anything and then they did nothing much. The whole world knew it had happened, but our media thought that they could simply ignore it, that no pressure would come from anywhere. Where did the pressure eventually come from? It came from women marching in the street. That was all they could do. They had no other lever. Now I've spent quite a lot of energy thinking about this and talking about this. How can we get our agenda tabled for immediate attention? How do we decide on our agenda? How do we learn first to arrive at a consensus and then to apply pressure?

In Australia I found myself suggesting to women that they join the Country Women's Association (CWA). And they looked at me in astonishment. "You mean jam and Jerusalem and all that stuff?" In Australia the CWA has 20,000 members in 1,200 branches. It has very efficient networking and it is very good at raising funds. It is normally biddable, but when it decides to lose its temper, the government trembles.

What made the CWA lose its temper? It lost its temper about fracking for coal seam gas. The exploration permits gave the miners the right to enter properties and begin sinking holes to find out if fracking was an option or not. Most of the holes the miners sank were useless, but they put the landowners through tremendous misery. In Australia many people have joined in a campaign called Lock the Gate. They imagine that you're allowed to "lock the gate" and keep the miners from using their exploration permits on your land. Legally you can't do that because the minerals belong to the Crown (no surprise to Canadians). What happens if you refuse to let the miners in? Miners can't legally break open your gate, but you can't keep them out either, and you can be forced by a court order to let them in. Then when they come to negotiate with you for the right to sink holes all over the place, you will be identified as hostile. The worst thing is that the Australian government has allowed the miners to treat negotiations with landholders as confidential. Miners are privileged. So that if the man next door has let the miners in for fifty thousand dollars a hole, you don't know anything about it, so you might let them in for five thousand dollars a hole. So, you wonder, whom is the government for? And the answer is the *miners*, that's whom it's for. So what made a difference? The CWA mobilized. It started shouting instead of speaking in a ladylike way. And the government trembled.

You all know, I hope, whereof I speak. The duly elected government of Quebec imposed a moratorium on shale gas mining and the US Lone Pine energy company is suing the provincial government of Quebec for $250 million. This is *force majeure*—this is what we are up against.

The Australian CWA is part of the ACWW, Associated Countrywomen of the World, which has more than nine million members in seventy countries. The ACWW has special consultative status with UNESCO. You should be proud that the Women's Institute movement was started in Canada, at Stoney Creek, Ontario, in 1897; by 1905 there were 130 branches in Ontario alone. In 1915, British women caught on. It was a Canadian, Madge Watt, who founded the Associated Countrywomen of the World in 1930. This is all part of the story that the Museum of Human Rights exists to tell.

No one ever embarrassed Tony Blair, except the Women's Institute. Blair came in to the national conference of British Women's Institutes in 2000 thinking he could charm them with boyish grins and funny little sexist innuendos, but they began banging the tables and heckling him and he was terrified. In the end he simply ran away. It didn't get the women anywhere. But it did prove something, that we women can work together in a pinch; we just have to do more of it, much more of it, more often.

You can say that it's great that women can have equal pay, and I'll say yeah, for twice as much work. They can earn two-thirds of what a man earns in a lifetime, isn't that just dandy? Doing jobs they don't want to do, jobs that have no career structure, jobs that have no future, jobs they have no choice about doing because they have to service the family debt. All of that is presented to us as wins in the struggle for women's rights. Why surely the struggle is over? You've won it all. You've gotten what you wanted. Really? We never defined what we wanted. It's always presented as if the lives led by men were the lives we wanted to lead.

In Australia what's just happened is that everything has been cut back, especially the care budget, the care of older people, who are mostly female and cared for by people who are mostly female. All pared back to the bone. And we've just bought fifty-eight fighter aircraft for twelve billion dollars. What do we think we're doing with them? We want a seat on the UN Security Council. No we don't! We want our older people to live their lives in reasonable dignity and not to be dying of thirst in our care homes. Not to be dying of hunger. Not to be dying of desperation and loneliness. If we want to change that agenda then we've got to do the thing I'm talking about. We've got to study power. We've got to actually see how we build up that pressure. How we get a cutting edge and how to apply it to a political system. How we change the agenda. We don't want to be allowed to vote for somebody else's agenda. We want a new agenda.

INDEX